VOICES

DAVID BOHLKE

**NATIONAL
GEOGRAPHIC**
LEARNING

Australia · Brazil · Canada · Mexico · Singapore · United Kingdom · United States

National Geographic Learning,
a Cengage Company

Voices Workbook 1, 1st Edition
David Bohlke

Publisher: Andrew Robinson

Managing Editor: Derek Mackrell

Director of Global Marketing: Ian Martin

Heads of Regional Marketing:

Charlotte Ellis (Europe, Middle East, and Africa)

Irina Pereyra (Latin America)

Justin Kaley (Asia)

Joy MacFarland (U.S. and Canada)

Product Marketing Manager: Caitlin Thomas

Production Manager: Daisy Sosa

Media Researcher: Leila Hishmeh

Art Director: Brenda Carmichael

Operations Support: Hayley Chwazik-Gee

Manufacturing Manager: Mary Beth Hennebury

Audio Producer: NY Audio

Composition: Composure

> For permission to use material from this text or product,
> submit all requests online at **cengage.com/permissions**
> Further permissions questions can be emailed to
> **permissionrequest@cengage.com**

Workbook:
ISBN: 978-0-357-44355-2

National Geographic Learning
200 Pier 4 Boulevard
Boston, MA 02110
U.S.A.

Locate your local office at **international.cengage.com/region**

Visit National Geographic Learning online at **ELTNGL.com**
Visit our corporate website at **www.cengage.com**

Printed in the United States Print
Number: 02 Print Year: 2023

Contents

1 Hello!

Vocabulary

Countries

1 Complete the crossword with countries.

Reading

1 Read the article. Write the correct city or country on the map on page 5.

2 Read the article again. Correct the mistakes.

1 Charlotte is from **Toronto**, Canada.

Charlotte is from Montreal, Canada.

2 **Dallan** is from Sweden.

_____

3 Bianca is from **Brazil**.

_____

4 Kiet is from **Bangkok**, Thailand.

_____

3 Read the article again. Complete each sentence with a word from the article.

1 _____*Beatrice*_____ is from Toronto.

2 Montreal is a _____ in Canada.

3 _____ is the capital city of Peru.

4 _____ is from Bangkok, Thailand.

Pronunciation

Stressing syllables

1 🔊 **1.1** Listen. Match these places to the places with similar word stress (1–6).

Toronto	Japan	Lima
Argentina	Vietnam	Washington

1 Montre**al**	3 Bra**zil**	5 Barce**lo**na
Vietnam	_____	_____
2 **Ken**ya	4 Hel**sin**ki	6 **Ca**nada
_____	_____	_____

2 🔊 **1.1** Listen again and repeat.

Look at the Learning to Learn box. Then do the task.

LEARNING TO LEARN: PRONUNCIATION

Counting syllables
Clap your hands to count the numbers of syllables in a word. Clap harder for syllables with stress.

Ken-ya [big clap] [little clap]

Look at the names of places (1–2). Clap to count the syllables. Then write the number of syllables.

1 Sweden _____

2 Finland _____

People and places

My name is Charlotte. I'm from Montreal. Montreal is a city in Canada. My best friend is Beatrice. She's from Toronto. It's in Canada, too.

My name is Dallan. I'm a scientist. I'm from Helsinki, Finland. My wife is Livvy. She's a scientist, too. She isn't from Finland. She's from Sweden.

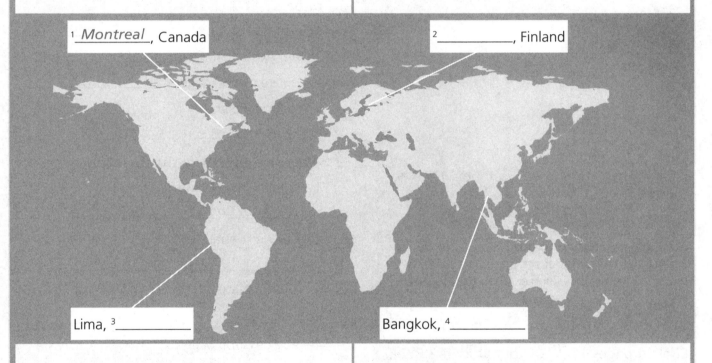

1 *Montreal*, Canada

2 _____, Finland

Lima, 3_____

Bangkok, 4_____

Hello. My name is Isabela. I'm from Lima. Lima is the capital city of Peru. My best friend is Bianca. She's in Brazil now, but she's from Peru, too.

My name is Pravat. I'm from Bangkok. Bangkok is a city in Thailand. My friend Kiet is from Chiang Mai. It's a city in Thailand, too.

Vocabulary

Nationalities

1 Circle the nationality in the rows of countries (1–5).

1 China (Korean) Greece Kenya

2 Japan Canada Vietnamese France

3 Indian Germany Brazil Turkey

4 Chile Bolivia Mexico Peruvian

5 Spain British Indonesia United States

2 Complete the nationalities.

1 Oman _i_

2 Morocc __ __

3 Fren __ __

4 Austral __ __ __

5 Japan __ __ __

6 Brazil __ __ __

Look at the Learning to Learn box. Then do the task.

LEARNING TO LEARN: VOCABULARY

Putting new words into groups

Put new words into groups to make it easier to remember them. For example, group nationalities by ...

- continent (Asia, Europe, South America, etc.)
- their word endings (Canad<u>ian</u>, Brazil<u>ian</u>, etc.)

Look at pages 14–15 of your Student's Book. Add one nationality to each group.

-n / an	*-ian*
American	Canadian
Moroccan	Brazilian
_____	_____

-ish	*-ese*	*other*
Turkish	Japanese	Omani
Polish	Chinese	Peruvian
_____	_____	_____

Grammar

Simple present *be* (singular, positive)

1 Choose the correct option to complete each sentence.

1 Ezio *am /is/ are* from Greece.

2 You *am / is / are* my best friend.

3 I *am / is / are* a scientist.

4 She *am / is / are* Kenyan.

5 It *am / is / are* from Brazil.

6 California *am / is / are* in the U.S.

2 Rewrite the sentences. Use the short form of *be*.

1 She is in France. *She's in France*_____.

2 I am Australian. _____.

3 You are a good singer. _____.

4 It is from Poland. _____.

5 I am from Mexico. _____.

3 Write sentences. Use the short form of *be*.

1 He / be / from China.

*He's from China.*_____

2 I / be / a scientist.

_____

3 You / be / in the U.K.

_____

4 She / be / from Athens.

_____

5 It / be / a city in Argentina.

_____

Grammar

Simple present *be* (singular, negative)

1 Match the sentence beginnings (1–4) with the endings (a–d).

1 I _____d_____   a not a scientist.

2 You _____   b aren't American.

3 She is _____   c isn't from Brazil.

4 He _____   d am not Vietnamese.

2 Complete the sentences with the negative form of *be.* Use short forms.

1 She ____*isn't*____ a teacher. She's a scientist.

2 I _____ American. I'm Canadian.

3 Madrid is in Spain. It _____ in France.

4 He's Omani. He _____ from Qatar.

5 You _____ a student here.

3 Complete the introductions with these words.

| I'm | It's | 's | isn't | isn't | isn't | She's |

I'm Klaus. I'm from Munich, Germany. My best friend is Tobias. He's from Salzburg. Salzburg ¹____*isn't*____ in Germany. ²_____ in Austria.

My name is Emilia. Nice to meet you! I'm a student. ³_____ from Antofagasta, Chile. My teacher ⁴_____ Chilean. ⁵_____ from Peru.

Hello. My name ⁶_____ Jason. I'm a singer from Canada. My wife is a singer, too. She ⁷_____ from Canada. She's from the United States.

Vocabulary

Numbers (0–10)

1 Write the numbers in word form.

8 _____*eight*_____

0 _____

3 _____

5 _____

2 _____

4 _____

6 _____

7 _____

1 _____

9 _____

10 _____

2 Complete the calculations. Write numbers in word form.

1 nine pens − two pens = _____*seven*_____ pens

2 three phones + five phones = _____ phones

3 _____ books − four books = three books

4 ten students − ten students = _____ students

5 two friends + _____ friends = six friends

Listening

1 🔊 **1.2** Listen to three conversations. What are they talking about? Circle the correct answers.

1 *a zip code / a phone number*

2 *a bank account number / an address*

3 *a phone number / a student number*

2 🔊 **1.2** Listen again. Write the numbers.

Conversation 1 _____

Conversation 2 _____

Conversation 3 _____

Grammar

Yes / No questions with *be* (singular)

1 Complete the questions. Use the correct form of *be*.

1 _____*Is*_____ Susan from Colombia?

2 _____ you from Barcelona?

3 _____ your address 66 Dairy Lane?

4 Excuse me. _____ I on West Street?

2 Complete the conversations with these words.

am	are	is	not

1 A: Is Danielle from France?

   B: Yes, she _____*is*_____.

2 A: Are you a scientist?

   B: No, I'm _____.

3 A: Are you Egyptian?

   B: Yes, I _____.

4 A: Am I in the right class?

   B: Yes, you _____.

Pronunciation

Stressing important words

1 🔊 **1.3** Listen and underline the stressed words.

1 I'm <u>Dana</u>. I'm from <u>Canada</u>.

2 I'm from Portugal. I'm not from Spain.

3 Are you French? I'm French, too.

2 🔊 **1.3** Listen again and repeat.

Writing

1 Read the profile. Circle the words that need capital letters. Write the corrections below.

Allie.J_99

Name:	(allie j.)	**Country:**	united states
Gender:	female	**City:**	los angeles
Nationality:	american	**Job:**	singer

1 *Allie J.*

2 _____

3 _____

4 _____

2 Match the pictures (1–5) with the words (a–e).

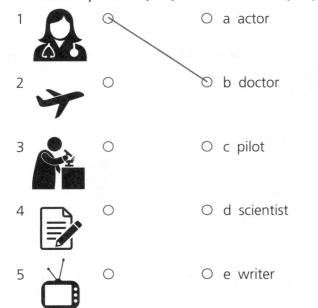

1   ○   ○ a actor

2   ○   ○ b doctor

3   ○   ○ c pilot

4   ○   ○ d scientist

5   ○   ○ e writer

3 Read the information. Complete the online profile. Use capital letters for people and place names only.

Hello! My name is Farouk. I'm a teacher at University of Granada, in Spain. I'm from Taroudant. Taroudant is a city in Morocco. Nice to meet you!

My profile
Name: ¹ *Farouk*_____   **Country:** ⁴_____
Gender: ²_____   **City:** ⁵_____
Nationality: ³_____   **Job:** ⁶_____

4 Check the profile. Use the checklist.

☐ Is the information correct?

☐ Is the spelling correct?

☐ Are the capital letters correct?

Look at the Learning to Learn box. Complete your learning journal.

LEARNING TO LEARN: YOUR LEARNING JOURNAL

Keep a learning journal. Write new words, phrases, and grammar notes in it. Practice your writing in it, too. Write in your journal often. You can write your journal:

• in a notebook.

• on your computer.

• on your phone or tablet.

Follow these steps to write new words in your journal:

1 Find a new word in your Student's Book.

2 Write a sentence from your Student's Book with the word in your journal.

3 Underline the new word.

For example:
Abbey is a <u>scientist</u>.
What <u>country</u> are you from?
My <u>address</u> is 2214 Smith Road.

1 Find these words in Unit 1 of your Student's Book. Copy the sentences with the words into your journal.

     name   nationality   meet

2 Find three more words in Unit 1. Write the words and sentences in your journal.

2 My home

Vocabulary

Rooms in a house

1 Complete the names of the rooms.

1 b _e_ _d_ _r_ o o _m_

2 __ i n __ __ g __ o o m

3 __ a t __ __ o __ m

4 __ __ v i n __ r __ __ m

5 __ i __ c __ __ n

2 Write the numbers (1–5) to match the words.

a bed _____   d couch _____

b dining table _____   e TV _____

c refrigerator _1_

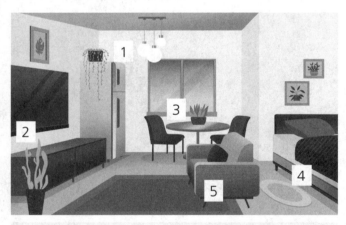

Look at the Learning to Learn box. Then do the task.

LEARNING TO LEARN: VOCABULARY

Labeling objects to learn new words

Label items at home to remember the words. Write the word on a piece of paper and put it on the item.

Find the English words for ten items in your home. Label the items.

Reading

1 Scan the article on page 11. What is not in Gabriela and Marco's house?

a a kitchen   d a living room

b a dining room   e bedrooms

c a bathroom

2 Look for the **bold** words in the article. Match the words with the pictures below. Then use a dictionary to check your answers.

a _roof_   c _____   e _____

b _____   d _____

3 Read the article. Are the sentences true (T) or false (F)?

1 Containers are metal boxes.   T F

2 People put things in containers.   T F

3 Container houses are cheap.   T F

4 Saxe uses new containers to build houses.   T F

5 Gabriela and Marco's house has five rooms.   T F

CONTAINER HOUSES

Container houses in Indonesia

Containers are large, **metal** boxes. People put things in these boxes and **send** them to other cities or countries. But containers are great for another thing: houses.

Benjamín García Saxe is from San José, Costa Rica. He **designs** container houses. He puts two or three containers together. Then he **cuts** a space for the windows and doors, and puts a **roof** on top.

Saxe's houses are large, but they're cheap and easy to build. They're also good for the environment because Saxe uses old containers to make them.

Gabriela Calvo and Marco Peralta live in a container house. It has a living room, a kitchen, a bathroom, and two bedrooms. Gabriela and Marco are very happy with their home.

A container on a truck

11

Grammar

Simple present *be* (plural, positive and negative)

1 Write sentences. Use short forms of *be*.

1 They / be / at school.

They're at school.

2 We / be / not / on the couch.

_____

3 You / be / at home.

_____

4 They / be / in the house.

_____

5 We / be / in the kitchen.

_____

6 They / be / not / on the dining table.

_____

2 Complete the conversations with *we're,* *you're,* or *they're.*

1 A: Hello. Are you Ying and Maya?

B: Um, no, [1]_____ *we're* _____ not.

[2]_____ over there.

A: OK, thanks!

2 A: Hi, Madison. Are Inga and I early?

B: No, [3]_____ not.

[4]_____ late.

A: Oh, no. Sorry!

3 A: Where are Paula and Victor?

B: [5]_____ in Room 3C.

A: Where are we?

B: [6]_____ in Room 3A.

Grammar

Yes / No questions with *be* (plural)

1 Change the sentences into *Yes / No* questions.

1 We're in the living room.

Are we in the living room _____?

2 They're under the table.

_____?

3 You're in the kitchen.

_____?

4 They're in the refrigerator.

_____?

5 We're next to the school.

_____?

6 You're at the bus station.

_____?

2 Write positive (+) or negative (−) short answers for the questions.

1 Are my friends and I late? (+)

Yes, you are.

2 Are Ben and Jesse at school? (+)

_____

3 Are you and Brandon at home? (+)

_____

4 Are the books under the table? (−)

_____

5 Are you and Ian in the library? (−)

_____

6 Are Tina, Cliff, and I early? (−)

_____

Pronunciation

Saying contractions of *be*

1 🔊 **2.1** **Listen. What words do you hear? Circle a or b.**

1 a I am   b I'm
2 a You are   b You're
3 a He is   b He's
4 a She is   b She's
5 a It is   b It's
6 a We are   b We're
7 a They are   b They're

2 🔊 **2.1** **Listen again and repeat.**

Vocabulary

Places in town

1 **Look at the puzzle. Find and circle ten places in town.**

```
K H B Z P B S H U B
Z M M D A Z U T T I
O U O C R L P L R Q
Y S V S K Z E M A L
O E I C D S R I I L
S U E H R T M F N I
U M T O N T A M S B
R D H O M D R A T R
N C E L U T K L A A
Q D A E K K E L T R
F O T P L V T O I Y
M Y E B Z V M K O M
O N R I F T I X N A
R E S T A U R A N T
B U S S T A T I O N
```

2 **Write the words from Exercise 1 next to the pictures.**

1   *mall*

2   _____

3   _____

4   _____

5   _____

6    _____

7   _____

8   _____

9 _____

10 _____

Listening

1 [🔊 2.2] Read the questions. Then listen to a video call between Idris and Celia. Number the questions in the order you hear them.

a _____ Where's Veracruz?

b _____ Who's Antonia?

c _____ Where are you?

d __1__ How are you?

2 [🔊 2.2] Listen again. Choose the correct option to complete each sentence.

1 Celia lives in a *house* / (an apartment.)

2 Celia is in her *bedroom* / *living room*.

3 The kitchen is *small* / *big*.

4 Antonia is a *friend* / *teacher*.

5 Antonia is from *Veracruz* / *Vietnam*.

Grammar

Who, what, where

1 Complete the questions with *who*, *what*, or *where*.

1 _____Who_____ is that?

2 _____ is the bus station?

3 _____ is that?

4 _____ are you?

Pronunciation

Understanding intonation in questions

1 [🔊 2.3] Listen to sentences 1–6. Are they statements or questions? Check (✓) the correct answer.

	statement	question
1	☐	☑
2	☐	☐
3	☐	☐
4	☐	☐
5	☐	☐
6	☐	☐

Writing

1 Complete the email with these phrases.

Write soon   I'm well   Hello   How are you

New Message

From: afonso567@flymail.com

To: paulodasilva8@mailme.com

Subject: A new apartment!

¹ _____Hello_____!

² _____? ³ _____. I'm in my new apartment here in Lisbon. It's small, but it's nice. It has a kitchen, a bathroom, a living room, and a bedroom. It's near the train station, so it's easy to go to college now. It's also next to a nice park.

How's college? And how's your new apartment?
⁴ _____!
Afonso

---

2 Read the email again. Circle the correct answer (a or b).

1 What is the email about?
  a a new school   ⓑ a new apartment

2 Who is the sender?
  a Paulo   b Afonso

3 Where is Afonso?
  a Brazil   b Lisbon

4 How many rooms are in Afonso's apartment?
  a four   b five

3 Read the email again. Choose a different subject line for the email.

a Welcome to Lisbon!

b My big apartment!

c My new home!

d See you soon!

4 Reply to Afonso's email. Use the notes below to help you. Write 30–40 words.

• Start your email with a friendly greeting.

• Answer Afonso's questions.

• Ask Afonso one or two questions.

• End your email in a friendly way.

5 Check your email. Use the checklist.

☐ Are the spelling and punctuation correct?

☐ Are the grammar and vocabulary correct?

☐ Does your email include all the information from the notes in Exercise 4?

Look at the Learning to Learn box. Then do the task.

LEARNING TO LEARN: USING A DICTIONARY

What does a word mean? How do you say it? Use a dictionary! Dictionaries are great when you don't know a word.

Dictionaries help answer these questions.

• How many meanings of the word are there?

• Which meaning is the one you want?

• Is the word a noun, a verb, or something else?

• How do you pronounce the word?

Some dictionaries also show how to use the word in a sentence.

present¹ (noun) /'preznt/ a gift
e.g., *A book is a nice present.*
present² (verb) /prɪˈzent/ to show something
e.g., *I presented my results to the group.*

Look at the words in the box. Use your own dictionary or an online dictionary and follow the steps (1–3).

date   watch   scarf

1 Check the meaning of the words in a dictionary.

2 Practice pronouncing the words.

3 Add the words to your learning journal.

1 & 2 Review 1

Vocabulary

1 Complete the numbers.

1 o _n_ e   7 f i __ __

2 s i __   8 t __ r __ e

3 t __ o   9 e i __ __ t

4 t e __   10 s __ v e __

5 n __ n __   11 __ e __ o

6 f o __ r

2 Complete the table with a country or nationality.

Country	Nationality
India	_Indian_
Vietnam	
Brazil	
	Japanese

3 Circle the correct option to complete each sentence.

1 The dining table is in the *bedroom* / (*dining room*)

2 The *refrigerator* / *shower* is in the bathroom.

3 The bed is in the *bedroom* / *dining room*.

4 The *shower* / *couch* is in the living room.

4 Complete the sentences with these words.

books   students   supermarkets   trees

1 _Students_ go to school.

2 You go to the library to get _____.

3 Parks have many _____.

4 People buy food from _____.

Grammar

1 Complete the conversations. Use the correct form of *be*. Use short forms when possible.

1 A: [1]_____ *Are* _____ (be) you from China?

    B: Yes, I [2]_____ (be).

2 A: [3]_____ (be) Tom in class?

    B: No, he [4]_____ (be / not).

3 A: [5]_____ (be) they Canadian?

    B: No. They [6]_____ (be) American.

4 A: [7]_____ (be) we late?

    B: No, you [8]_____ (be / not).

2 Choose the correct options to complete the conversation.

[1]*What* / (*Where*) are you???

> We're on the bus. Are we late?

Yes, you are. 😕 [2]*Who* / *What* are you with?

> I'm with Jason and his friend.

Jason's friend? [3]*What's* / *Who's* his name?

> Enrique.

Oh. Is he Jason's friend from Spain?

> Yes, he is. OK, I'm at the bus station. [4]*Where* / *Who* are you?

At the restaurant next to the movie theater. Hurry!

Reading

1 Read the poster below. What is it about? Check (✓) the correct answer.

a students ☐ b classes ☐ c teachers ☐

WELCOME!	Port Charles College

Say "hello" to our three new students

Name: Omar Abboud

From: Sohag, Egypt

Hello! I'm Omar. I'm from Sohag. It's a small city in Egypt. It's a nice place. I'm a teacher in Egypt, but I'm a student here. It's nice to meet you!

Name: Cristina Russo

From: Novara, Italy

Hi! My name is Cristina. I'm Italian. I'm from Novara. It's a small city near Milan. My favorite place here is the library. The park is really nice, too!

Name: Nikki Johnson

From: Caledon, Canada

Hello everyone. I'm Nikki. I'm from Caledon. It's a small town near Toronto. My new house here is lovely! It's on Smith Street, near the museum.

2 Complete the diagram. Write the letters (a–f).

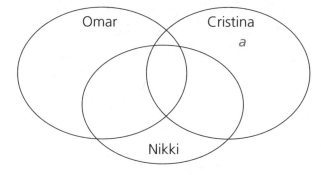

a Italian
b teacher
c student
d from a city
e from a town
f female

Listening

1 🎧 R1.1 Listen to Wendy talk about her home. Which photo is it? ___

2 🎧 R1.1 Listen again. Correct the mistake in each sentence.

1 Wendy's home is next to a **museum**.

Wendy's home is next to a park.

2 Her home is near the **train station**.

_____

3 Her home has **four** rooms.

_____

4 Her home has no dining room or **bathroom**.

_____

5 Her bed is in the **kitchen**.

_____

Pronunciation

1 🎧 R1.2 Listen. <u>Underline</u> the syllable with more stress.

1 <u>ci</u>-ty   4 mu-se-um
2 sho-wer   5 su-per-mar-ket
3 sta-tion   6 af-ter-noon

2 🎧 R1.3 Listen and circle the word you hear.

1 (it is)   it's
2 who is   who's
3 is not   isn't
4 we are   we're

3 My stuff

Vocabulary

Travel items

1 Match 1–6 with a–f to make travel items. Then write the words.

1 ATM	a bottle	_____
2 note	b brush	_____
3 pass	c book	_____
4 T-	d port	_____
5 water	e shirt	_____
6 tooth	f card	_ATM card_

2 Look at the pictures. Complete the crossword.

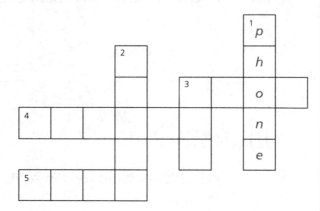

Down

1
2
3

Across

3
4
5

Reading

1 Scan Kelly's message to Dan on page 19. Circle the commas and the word *and*. How many things does Kelly ask Dan to pack? _____

2 Circle the items Kelly asks Dan to pack.

an ATM card	a book	a camera	a dress
a laptop	a notebook	a passport	a pen
a cellphone	T-shirts	a water bottle	

3 Read the two messages on page 19. Correct the mistakes.

1 Kelly's travel bag is **black**.

   Kelly's travel bag is brown. _____

2 Kelly's travel bag is **small**.

   _____.

3 Kelly needs **three** T-shirts.

   _____.

4 Dan doesn't know where Kelly's **camera** is.

   _____.

4 Choose the correct option to complete the sentences.

1 The bag is *next to / on / under* the bed.

2 The dress is *on / next to / under* the bed.

3 The notebook is *in / on / next to* the TV.

Help me pack!

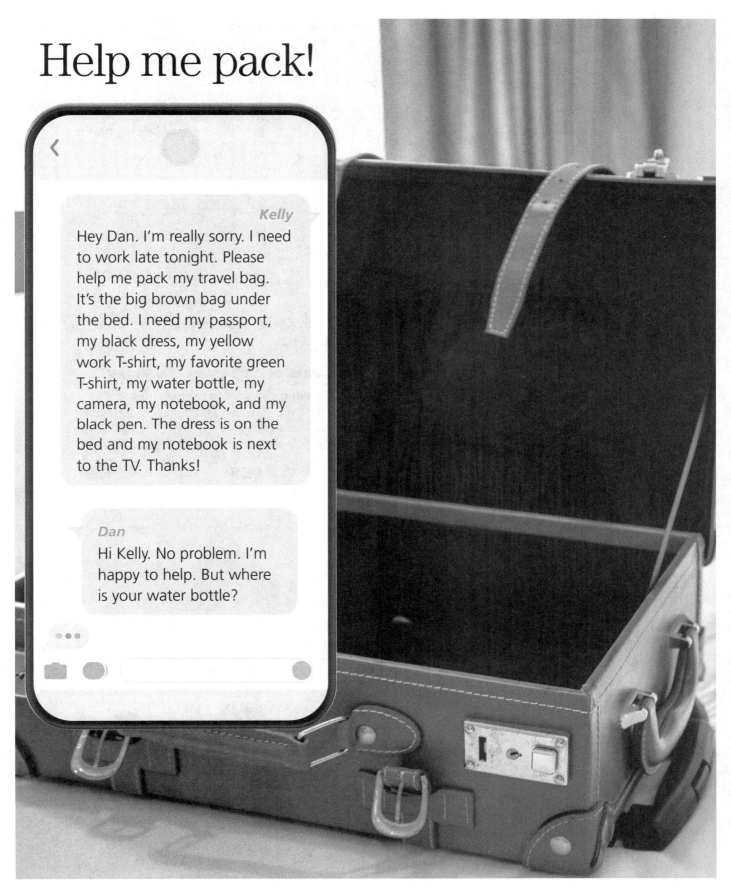

Kelly

Hey Dan. I'm really sorry. I need to work late tonight. Please help me pack my travel bag. It's the big brown bag under the bed. I need my passport, my black dress, my yellow work T-shirt, my favorite green T-shirt, my water bottle, my camera, my notebook, and my black pen. The dress is on the bed and my notebook is next to the TV. Thanks!

Dan

Hi Kelly. No problem. I'm happy to help. But where is your water bottle?

Grammar

This, that, these, those

1 Complete the questions with *this, that, these,* or *those.*

1 What are ___*those*___?

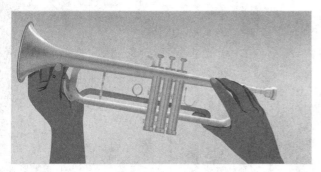

2 What's _____?

3 What's _____?

4 What are _____?

2 Circle the correct options to complete the conversations.

1 A: ¹*This /* (*These*) are my keys.

   B: Are they?

   A: Yes. ²*This / Those* are your keys on the table.

2 A: What's ³*that / those* in your hand?

   B: Oh, ⁴*this / these* is my new camera.

   A: It's very nice!

3 A: What are ⁵*this / those*?

   B: They're old coins. ⁶*That / These* one is from Turkey.

   A: How interesting!

Look at the Learning to Learn box. Then do the task.

LEARNING TO LEARN: GRAMMAR

Drawing pictures to learn grammar

When you learn new grammar, it's sometimes helpful to draw pictures. For example, the pictures below show how to use *this, that, these,* and *those*.

	NEAR	**FAR**
ONE	THIS 	THAT 
TWO OR MORE	THESE 	THOSE 

Draw four pictures to show these sentences (1–4).

1 *This is a cellphone.*   3 *These are coins.*

2 *That is a bag.*   4 *Those are keys.*

Pronunciation

Saying /ð/

1 🔊 3.1 Listen and number the words in the order you hear them.

a _____ this   d __1__ that

b _____ these   e _____ those

c _____ they   f _____ the

2 🔊 3.1 Listen again and repeat.

Vocabulary

Colors

1 Complete the colors.

1 r e _d_

2 b l __ e

3 p __ __ k

4 __ e l l o __

5 w __ i __ e

6 p u __ p __ e

7 o __ a n __ e

8 __ r e __ n

9 b __ a c __

2 Check online. Match the sentence beginnings (1–4) with the endings (a–d).

1 South Korea's flag is _____c_____

2 Colombia's flag is _____

3 The Seychelles' flag is _____

4 Ireland's flag is _____

a green, white, and orange.

b yellow, blue, and red.

c red, black, white, and blue.

d blue, yellow, red, white, and green.

Listening

1 🔊 3.2 Listen to a conversation. Circle the colors you hear.

blue   pink   red
green   black   white
orange   yellow   purple

2 🔊 3.2 Listen again. Complete the sentences with colors.

1 Dani's car is _____pink_____.

2 Dani's favorite color is _____.

3 Jasmine's T-shirt in the photo of the car is _____ and _____.

4 Jasmine's favorite color is _____.

Look at the Learning to Learn box. Then do the task.

LEARNING TO LEARN: LISTENING

Watching videos to practice listening

Practice listening at home. Watch videos online with English subtitles. Read the words they say. Here are some tips.

These words are from my heart …

1 Choose a video with subtitles.

2 Watch the video two or three times. Listen and read the subtitles.

3 Turn off the subtitles. Then listen again.

Find and watch a video with English subtitles. Practice the tips in the Learning to Learn box.

Grammar

Possessive adjectives and 's

1 Complete the conversations. Use possessive adjectives.

1 A: Is that Adam's cellphone?

   B: No. _____*His*_____ cellphone is black.

2 A: Are those new students?

   B: Yes. _____ names are Ahmed and Khalid.

3 A: What's your favorite color, Quang?

   B: _____ favorite color is pink.

4 A: What color is Japan's flag?

   B: _____ flag is white and red.

5 A: What's _____ favorite city?

   B: Our favorite city is Amsterdam.

6 A: Are those Sarah's books?

   B: No. _____ books are in her bag.

2 Rewrite the sentences. Use 's.

1 Paul has an orange couch.

   Paul's couch is orange.

2 Laura has a black cellphone.

   _____

3 My friend has beautiful eyes.

   _____

4 Gina has a pink water bottle.

   _____

5 Ming has a blue and yellow house.

   _____

Pronunciation

Saying *your* and *their*

1 🎧 3.3 Listen and match 1–4 with a–d to make the correct sentences.

1 Your _____*c*_____   a house is white.

2 You're _____   b from India.

3 Their _____   c teacher is here.

4 They're _____   d late for school.

2 🎧 3.3 Listen again and repeat.

Writing

1 Read the social media post. Correct the four mistakes.

KeishaK_93

This is my new T-shirt. **Its** very special to **me** It's from my friend in the **u.k.** I love the words and the pictures on it. It's my new **favorit** T-shirt!

1 *It's* _____

2 _____

3 _____

4 _____

2 **Look at the photos and choose your favorite item of clothing below. Make notes for the questions (1–4).**

1 What is it? _____

2 Is it old or new? _____

3 Where is it from? _____

4 Why is it special? _____

T-shirt

jacket

scarf

hat

shoes

jeans

dress

sunglasses

3 **Write a social media post about your favorite item of clothing from Exercise 2. Use your notes to help you, and the post on page 22 as a model. Write 30–40 words.**

4 **Check your social media post. Use the checklist.**

☐ Are the spelling and punctuation correct?

☐ Are the grammar and vocabulary correct?

☐ Does your post include all the information from your notes in Exercise 2?

Look at the Learning to Learn box. Complete your learning journal.

LEARNING TO LEARN: YOUR LEARNING JOURNAL

It's good to write sentences from the Student's Book in your learning journal (see Unit 1). This helps you remember the words.

But there are other ways to write words in your learning journal. Here are some other ideas:

1 Draw a picture of the word.

Bag

2 Write the meaning of the word.
bag—You carry things in it.

3 Write your own sentence with the word to show what it means. For example:
I carry my bag to school every day.
This sentence shows the meaning of *bag*. It also explains *carry*.

1 Add these words to your learning journal. Use one of the ideas from the box (1–3) to help you remember the words.

guitar   money   far

2 Find five more words in Unit 3. Add them to your learning journal. Use the ideas from the box to help you remember the words.

4 Habits

Vocabulary

Numbers (11–100)

1 Write the numbers in word form.

1 _____seventy_____

4 _____

2 _____

5 _____

3 _____

6 _____

2 Write the times.

1 eleven thirty-five _____11:35_____

2 seven ten _____

3 twelve fifty-nine _____

Reading

1 Read the article on page 25. Match the cities (1–4) with the forms of transportation (a–d).

1 Copenhagen ___c___ 3 La Paz _____

2 Ho Chi Minh City _____ 4 Melbourne _____

a tram   b cable car   c bicycle   d motorcycle

2 Scan the article again. Complete the sentences with numbers.

1 About _____40_____% of the people in Copenhagen commute by bicycle.

2 About _____ million people live in Ho Chi Minh City.

3 A cable car ticket in La Paz costs about _____ cents.

4 There are about _____ tram cars in Melbourne.

3 Read the article again. Are the sentences true (T) or false (F)?

1 Most people in Copenhagen have a bicycle. T F

2 Motorcycles are expensive in Vietnam. T F

3 In La Paz, the waiting time for cable cars is very long. T F

4 Visitors to Melbourne like the city's trams. T F

Pronunciation

Saying /ʌ/

1 🔊 4.1 Listen and underline the /ʌ/ sound.

1 b<u>u</u>s stop   3 money   5 under

2 number   4 hundred   6 running

Commuting around the world

People around the world commute to work. Some walk, some drive, and some take the bus or train. Here are some ways people get to work.

Copenhagen, Denmark

This city is very bike-friendly. About 90% of the people there have a bicycle, and over 40% of commuters go to work or school by bicycle. The city has 400 kilometers of bike paths.

Ho Chi Minh City, Vietnam

About nine million people live in this city, and about 70% of them go to work or school by motorcycle. People like motorcycles because they're good for short trips and they aren't expensive.

La Paz, Bolivia

Many commuters here travel by cable car. Tickets are cheap (about 3 bolivianos, or 44 cents) and the views are amazing. The waiting time is short. A new cable car comes every 15 seconds.

Melbourne, Australia

This city is famous for its trams. Many people use them to get to work or school. Melbourne has 24 tram lines and about 490 tram cars. Melbourne's trams are famous. They are popular with people from Melbourne and tourists.

Grammar

Simple present

1 Circle the correct options to complete the texts.

1 Fatima ¹*go /*(*goes*)to bed at 11:30. She ²*wake / wakes* up at 4:30. She ³*don't / doesn't* sleep a lot.

2 Martin ⁴*have / has* three cats. The cats ⁵*don't / doesn't* sleep at night. They ⁶*sleep / sleeps* in the day.

3 Ling ⁷*work / works* at night. She ⁸*starts / start* work at 11 p.m. and ⁹*finish / finishes* at 7 a.m. Then she ¹⁰*go / goes* home and ¹¹*sleep / sleeps*.

4 Steven and Zoe ¹²*live / lives* in Dublin. Steven ¹³*work / works* at a museum. Zoe doesn't ¹⁴*work / works*. She ¹⁵*study / studies* at a university.

2 Complete the sentences. Use the correct form of the verbs in parentheses.

My sister and I ¹___*study*___ (study) at the same university. Our classes ²_____ (not / start) at the same time. My classes ³_____ (begin) in the afternoon. At 12 p.m., I ⁴_____ (take) the bus to university. I ⁵_____ (read) a book on the bus. My sister's classes are in the morning. The mornings are cool, so she ⁶_____ (ride) her bicycle to class every day. It's a long trip, but she ⁷_____ (love) the exercise!

Grammar

Simple present questions and answers

1 Match the questions (1–5) with the answers (a–e).

1 What time do you get up? ___*b*___

2 Do you sleep a lot? _____

3 Does your friend walk to class? _____

4 Do your friends take the bus? _____

5 Where does your father work? _____

a At a school.

b At 7:30.

c Yes, I do.

d Yes, she does.

e No, they don't.

2 Complete the conversations with the correct words.

1 A: ¹_____*Do*_____ you sleep a lot?

  B: Yes, I ²_____.

  A: How many hours do you sleep?

  B: I ³_____ ten hours a day.

2 A: ⁴_____ your friends walk to school?

  B: No, they ⁵_____.

  A: How ⁶_____ they go to school?

  B: They take a bus.

3 A: When ⁷_____ your father start work?

  B: He ⁸_____ work at 6:00 p.m.

  A: Does he work all night?

  B: No, he ⁹_____.

Look at the Learning to Learn box. Then do the task.

LEARNING TO LEARN: GRAMMAR

Writing true sentences
Use new grammar to write true sentences about you. Write a positive (+) sentence. Then write a negative (–) sentence. For example:

I go to bed at 11:00 p.m. (positive)

I don't go to bed at 8:00 p.m. (negative)

Write two true sentences for each question (one positive, one negative).

1 What time does your class start?

_____

_____

2 When do you get home?

_____

_____

Vocabulary

Days of the week

1 Look at Jessie's calendar. Write the days.

Monday	go to the supermarket
Tuesday	play tennis with Sean
Wednesday	study for math test
Thursday	MATH TEST!!
Friday	–
Saturday	have dinner with sister
Sunday	meet Carla for lunch

When does Jessie …

1 play tennis with Sean? _____Tuesday_____

2 have dinner with her sister? _____

3 study for her math test? _____

4 have no plans? _____

5 meet Carla for lunch? _____

6 go to the supermarket? _____

7 take her math test? _____

2 Complete the sentences with the correct day of the week.

1 The day before Tuesday is _____Monday_____.

2 The day before Friday is _____.

3 The day before Monday is _____.

4 The day after Tuesday is _____.

5 The day after Thursday is _____.

6 The day between Monday and Wednesday is

_____.

7 The day between Friday and Sunday is

_____.

Listening

1 🎧 4.2 Listen to Nadia interview her father for a homework assignment. Are the sentences true (T) or false (F)?

1 Nadia's father walks to work.　　　　　T　F

2 Nadia's father usually exercises　　　　T　F
after lunch on Saturday.

3 Nadia's father has dinner with　　　　　T　F
his friends on Saturday.

4 Nadia usually has dinner with　　　　　T　F
her parents on Sunday night.

2 🎧 4.2 Listen again. Complete the sentences with *always, usually, sometimes,* or *never.*

1 Nadia's father _____usually_____ works on Saturdays.

2 Nadia's parents _____ have lunch together on Saturdays.

3 Nadia's parents _____ watch a movie on Saturday evening.

4 Nadia's father _____ gets up early on Sunday.

Grammar

Adverbs of frequency

1 Choose the correct option to complete each sentence.

1 *Never I'm /* (*I'm never*) late for English class.

2 Jeanne *usually walks / walks usually* to school.

3 Ben *always is / is always* at work before 9 p.m.

4 Yumiko *never studies / studies never* on the weekend.

5 Allie *is usually / usually is* at the park on Friday.

2 Rewrite the sentences. Correct the mistakes with word order.

1 Damien and I study **usually** at the library.
   *Damien and I **usually** study at the library.*

2 **Never** my father works on weekends.
   _____

3 Teresa takes the train **always** to work.
   _____

4 I am late **sometimes** for class.
   _____

3 How often do you do these things? Write sentences that are true for you. Use adverbs of frequency.

1 go to bed before 11 p.m.
   I usually go to bed before 11 p.m.

2 speak English outside of class
   _____

3 watch music videos online
   _____

4 read English newspapers
   _____

Pronunciation

Saying /juː/

1 🎧 **4.3** Listen. Circle the words with a /juː/ sound.

1 (huge)   3 music   5 umbrella

2 excuse   4 Sunday   6 university

2 🎧 **4.3** Listen again and repeat the words with a /juː/ sound.

Writing

1 Put the words in order.

1 free / you / are / ?
   Are you free?
   _____

2 well / I / all / hope / is / .
   _____

3 me / know / let / .
   _____

4 I'm / this week / Frankfurt / in / .
   _____

5 to meet / with you / I'd like / .
   _____

2 Put the sentences from Exercise 1 in the correct order to write an email.

Hi,

_____

_____

_____

_____

Sincerely,
Bryan

3 What do you think about the tone of Bryan's email? Is it friendly and professional?

_____

4 Make notes to reply to Bryan's email. Think about the following things.

- What days are you busy next week?

- What days are you free next week?

- What date and time would you like to meet?

- What else would you like to say to Bryan?

5 Write a reply to Bryan's email. Use your notes from Exercise 4 to help you. Write 35–40 words.

- Use a polite greeting.

- Say something friendly at the start of your email.

- Say when you are busy.

- Say when you are free.

- Say when you would like to meet.

- End your email in a polite way.

6 Check your email. Use the checklist.

☐ Are the spelling and punctuation correct?

☐ Are the grammar and vocabulary correct?

☐ Does your email include all the information from the notes in Exercise 5?

Look at the Learning to Learn box. Then do the tasks.

LEARNING TO LEARN: MANAGING YOUR TIME

Learning a language takes time and students often have busy lives. That's why it's important to manage your time well. Think about what you want to learn and how much time you have.

1 Complete the sentences with *always, usually, sometimes,* or *never.*

I _____ make a list of things I want or need to learn.

I _____ finish all my English homework.

I _____ find time to practice English with friends.

I _____ write new words and language in my learning journal.

I _____ read my learning journal and try to remember new words.

2 Make a plan. Follow these steps.

1 Look at the sentences with *never* or *sometimes.*

2 Think about why you don't do these things often.

3 Make a plan to do these things.

3 & 4 Review 2

Vocabulary

1 Complete the travel items.

When I travel, I pack these things: my
¹t o __ t h __ r u __ h, my ²c __ m e __ a, my
³__ a __ e r bottle, some ⁴T - s __ i __ t s, and a
⁵d r __ __ s or two. I put them all in my travel
⁶b __ g. My most important travel item is my
⁷p a __ __ p o __ t.

2 Check online. Write the six colors of the Olympic flag.

_____white_____ _____ _____

_____ _____ _____

3 Write the time in word form.

1 1:26 _one twenty-six_____

2 7:58 _____

3 12:49_____

4 11:14_____

4 Read the sentences. Are they true (T) or false (F)?

1 One hour is 60 seconds.   T F

2 One week is seven days.   T F

3 Tomorrow is after today.   T F

4 Sunday is one day after Monday.   T F

Grammar

1 Correct the mistake in each sentence.

1 **That** are my clothes on the bed over there.
   Those are my clothes on the bed over there.

2 This isn't my father's bag. **Her** bag is black.

   _____

3 **Johns** best friend is from Hungary.

   _____

4 The cat is white, but **their** feet are black.

   _____

5 Come here and look. **These** is my new laptop.

   _____

2 Circle the correct options to complete the conversations.

1 A: ⓘDo / Does you work near here?

   B: No. I ²work / works at the university.

2 A: Do they ³drive / drives to work?

   B: No. They ⁴take / takes the bus.

3 A: Does your class ⁵start / starts at 9:00?

   B: Yes. And it ⁶finish / finishes at 10:30.

4 A: Where ⁷do / does he study?

   B: He ⁸studies sometimes /
      sometimes studies at the library.

5 A: Why is ⁹always she / she always tired?

   B: She ¹⁰doesn't / don't sleep a lot.

Reading

1 Read the article. When does Tracy do these things? Match the activities (1–4) with the times (a–d).

1 study   __c__   a at night

2 teach   _____   b in the evening

3 play video games   _____   c in the afternoon

4 watch movies   _____   d in the morning

2 Complete the sentences with words from the article.

1 Tracy studies from Monday to ___Friday___.

2 Tracy's students are from _____.

3 Tracy sometimes plays video games with _____.

4 Tracy usually watches movies and _____.

My life online

My name is Tracy, and I'm a student. My weekdays are usually busy. I study from Monday to Friday, in the afternoon.

I work as a teacher on weekdays, too. I teach English online to students in Korea. I live in London, so class starts early for me, at 8:30 a.m. But for my students, class starts at 5:30 p.m.

I usually rest a lot on the weekend. Sometimes, I play video games online with my friend Mateo. We usually play in the evening, at around 6 p.m. At night, I usually watch movies and TV shows.

Listening

1 🎧 R2.1 Listen to an interview with Charlene about her hobby. Number the questions in the order you hear them.

A woman with a metal detector

a _____ Is it an expensive hobby?

b _____ Why do you like this hobby?

c _____ When do you go out?

d ___1___ Where do you go to look for things?

2 🎧 R2.1 Listen again. Circle the correct answer (a or b).

1 What does Charlene usually find?

   a wallets and old phones

   (b) keys and drink cans

2 When does she look for things?

   a Saturday mornings   b Sunday mornings

3 Why does she like her hobby?

   a She finds money.   b She helps people.

Pronunciation

1 🎧 R2.2 Listen and write the sentences.

1 _____.

2 _____.

2 🎧 R2.3 Listen and circle the sound you hear.

1 run (/ʌ/) /juː/   4 future /ʌ/ /juː/

2 you /ʌ/ /juː/   5 lunch /ʌ/ /juː/

3 fun /ʌ/ /juː/   6 music /ʌ/ /juː

5 Inside or outside?

Reading

1 Scan the poster on page 33. Choose another title (a or b).

   a I never upcycle. Here's why.

   b Don't recycle clothes. Upcycle!

2 Read the article again. Complete the table with items from the poster.

Old items	New items
skateboard	
	flowerpots

Look at the Learning to Learn box. Then do the task.

LEARNING TO LEARN: READING

Making notes

When you read, think about these questions:

   1 What is the main idea?

   2 Are there any new words?

   3 What words or ideas are important?

Make notes on your text when you read.

Start an online book club! Ask   *main idea*
some friends to join your club. Pick
a book to read. Then talk about it.
A different club member chooses the   *important*
next book and <u>hosts</u> the club.   *new word*

Make notes on the poster on page 33. Are there words, sentences, or ideas you don't understand? Use a dictionary to find out what they mean.

Vocabulary

Common activities

1 Choose the correct words to make activities.

   1 watch *a book / a song /* (TV)

   2 chat *a friend / online / internet*

   3 sing *a friend / a song / TV*

   4 play *dance / exercise / a video game*

   5 listen to *music / a picture / dance*

   6 draw *music / a picture / a book*

2 Match the pictures with the activities (1–6) from Exercise 1.

a

d

b

e

c

f

3 Complete the sentences with information that is true for you. Use the activities from Exercise 1.

   1 I sometimes _____.

   2 I never _____.

   3 I _____ every day.

Do you upcycle?

We all know what recycling is. Many of us recycle paper, plastic, and metal. But what about upcycling? Upcycling is turning something old into something new and nice.

Need a place for your books? Build a shelf from a skateboard.

Paint old cans, along with plastic and glass bottles, to make chess pieces.

Paint old car tires different colors and use them as flowerpots.

Build a cat bed from an old piece of luggage.

Make bike racks from old car tires.

Other things to upcycle

Magazines

Clothes

Bottles and cans

Furniture

33

Grammar

Like, love, and *don't like* + *-ing* form

1 Complete the sentences with the correct simple present form of the verbs *like, love,* and *don't like*.

 love

 like

don't like

1 I _____love_____ playing basketball. 😍

2 Carrie _____ doing yoga. 🙁

3 Do you _____ playing tennis? 🙂

4 Hui _____ running and swimming. 🙂

5 Gustav and I _____ playing soccer. 🙁

6 My friends and I _____ camping. 😍

2 Put the words in order to make sentences and questions. Use the *-ing* form of the activities.

1 cycle / Isobel / loves / .

Isobel loves cycling.

2 don't like / swim / I / .

_____

3 they / do / climb / like / ?

_____

4 Kendra / do / doesn't like / yoga / .

_____

5 Ricardo / like / does / horseback ride / ?

_____

6 like / play / where / they / do / soccer / ?

_____

3 Write sentences that are true for you. Use *love, like,* or *don't like* and the words in parentheses.

1 I _____. (exercise)

2 My friends _____.
(play video games)

3 My friend _____.
(chat online)

Pronunciation

Saying /ŋ/

1 🎧 5.1 Listen and write the activities you hear.

1 ____playing____ 4 _____

2 _____ 5 _____

3 _____ 6 _____

2 🎧 5.1 Listen again and repeat.

Vocabulary

Months and seasons

1 Complete the calendar with the months.

January	February	
April		June

2 Match the seasons (1–4) with the words (a–d).

1 spring _____

2 summer _____

3 fall _____

4 winter _____

a cool then warm

b cold

c hot

d warm then cool

3 Write the correct season.

1 When are the nights long?

winter

2 When do flowers start to grow?

_____

3 When are the days long?

_____

4 When do leaves start to fall?

_____

Listening

1 🎧 5.2 **Listen to Cory and Mia make plans. Circle the activities they talk about.**

playing tennis   hiking

playing basketball   cycling

playing video games   swimming

2 🎧 5.2 **Read the questions. Think about what you need to listen for. Then listen again. Circle the correct answer (a or b).**

1 What does Mia not like doing?

  a playing video games   b playing basketball

2 Who is busy on Saturday afternoon?

  a Cory   b Mia

3 Why is 3 p.m. on Sunday a bad time for Cory?

  a He's at work.   b He's at school.

4 When do they agree to meet?

  a Saturday at 4 p.m.   b Sunday at 4 p.m.

5 Where do they plan to meet?

  a at the park   b at school

Grammar

Prepositions of time

1 Complete the table with these words.

spring	2022	night
Tuesday	Fridays	3:30 p.m.
February	the evening	the weekend

at	in	on
night	*spring*	*Fridays*

2 Complete the conversations with *at, in,* or *on*.

1 A: What do you usually do [1]_____ the afternoon?

   B: I study at the library.

   A: What do you do [2]_____ night?

   B: I meet my friends.

2 A: Do you want to see a movie [3]_____ Thursday?

   B: Sure. What time do you want to meet?

   A: Let's meet [4]_____ 7 p.m. at the movie theater.

   B: Perfect!

3 A: What do you like doing [5]_____ the summer?

   B: I love swimming.

   A: When do you usually swim?

   B: I go swimming [6]_ _ _____ the evening when it's cool.

Pronunciation

Understanding connected speech: *would you*

1 🔊 5.3 Listen. Is the person using connected speech? Write C when *would* and *you* are connected. Write N when they are not connected.

1 Who would you like to see?   _C_

2 What would you like to do?   _____

3 What would you like to eat?   _____

4 Where would you like to go?   _____

Writing

1 Choose the correct verb to make activities.

1 *play / go / (visit)* my parents

2 *try / help / make* snowboarding

3 *meet / learn / have* new people

4 *do / play / go* soccer

5 *read / help / buy* a new laptop

6 *learn / make / listen* to drive

7 *go / want / play* hiking

Look at the Learning to Learn box. Then do the task.

LEARNING TO LEARN: WRITING

Remembering new phrases

It's important to remember words that go together. For example, we say *go hiking* (not ~~do hiking~~) and *see the world* (not ~~watch the world~~). Write new phrases in your learning journal and try to remember them.

Look at the phrases in Exercise 1. Write the phrases in your journal.

2 Make notes. Think about your next work or school break. Answer the questions and complete the table.

1 How do you feel about your next break? (happy, excited, etc.)

2 When does it start? When does it end? (summer, November, etc.)

3 Do you have a lot of plans?

How I feel	
When it starts	
When it ends	

3 Think of six things you would like to do during your break. Complete the list below with your ideas. Begin each item with a verb. Write the six things in order. For example:

• by how important they are
• by how easy they are
• alphabetically

Six things I want to do	
1	
2	
3	
4	
5	
6	

4 Write about your next work or school break. Use your notes in Exercise 2 to write a short introduction. Then list the things you want to do from Exercise 3. Write 30–40 words.

5 Check your writing. Use the checklist.

☐ Are the spelling and punctuation correct?

☐ Are the grammar and vocabulary correct?

☐ Does your writing include all the information from your notes in Exercises 2 and 3?

Look at the Learning to Learn box. Then do the task.

LEARNING TO LEARN: YOUR LEARNING JOURNAL

Your learning journal is a great place to make notes on new grammar. As you learn new grammar, think about these questions:

1 What about the grammar is easy? (e.g., *Using the short form* I'm *for* I am.)

2 What about the grammar is difficult? (e.g., *Using the short form* isn't.)

3 What's important to remember about the grammar? (e.g., *Usually use short forms in conversations*.)

Add example sentences. Underline or highlight useful parts. For example:

I am	*I'm in Room 6.*
	I'm not in Room 6.
	Am I in Room 6?
He / She / It is	*She's from France.*
	She isn't from France.
	Is she from France?
We / You / They are	*They are at home.*
	They aren't at home.
	Are they at home?

Choose a grammar point from Units 1 to 5. Make notes about it in your journal.

6 Food around the world

Vocabulary

Food

1 Find and circle these words in the puzzle.

1 5 9

2 6 10

3 7 11

4 8 12

B	G	C	R	A	F	M	V
R	L	O	R	B	Y	I	L
E	K	F	T	V	P	L	Z
A	J	F	Y	E	A	K	A
D	H	E	G	G	S	F	Q
D	G	E	U	E	M	R	W
F	I	S	H	T	N	U	S
S	D	W	I	A	B	I	M
A	F	E	O	B	V	T	E
N	O	O	D	L	E	S	A
Q	C	H	E	E	S	E	T
R	I	C	E	S	T	E	A

2 Choose the correct options to complete the conversations.

1 A: Do you like milk in your coffee / *vegetables*?

   B: No, but I like sugar.

2 C: What do you drink for breakfast?

   D: I usually have *eggs / tea*.

Learning to Learn box

Look at the Learning to Learn box. Then do the task.

LEARNING TO LEARN: VOCABULARY

Building your vocabulary

There are many ways to learn new words outside of class. Here are some ideas.

• Use English to search online.

• Use vocabulary-learning apps.

• Watch TV shows or movies with English subtitles on.

Search online for "fruit." Add ten new types of fruit to your journal.

Reading

1 Skim the article on page 39. What is the article probably about? Check (✓) the correct answer.

a ☐ fast and easy breakfasts

b ☐ different egg dishes

c ☐ dinner around the world

2 Read the article again. Answer the questions.

1 Is egg drop soup from the U.K.?

_____

2 When do people eat egg drop soup?

_____

3 Where do people eat *loco moco*?

_____

4 Do people eat *loco moco* for lunch?

_____

5 What do people usually eat *shakshuka* with?

_____

Egg-citing dishes!

People around the world love eggs. Many people enjoy them for breakfast, but eggs are delicious any time of the day.

Egg drop soup is from China, but it's popular in the U.S., the U.K., and many other countries. The dish has eggs, chicken, onions, salt, and pepper. People usually eat it for lunch or dinner. It's cheap and it's easy to make.

Loco moco is a very popular dish in the U.S. state of Hawaii. It has white rice, meat, onions, salt, and pepper. There's always an egg on top. People usually have it for breakfast, but it's also a popular dish for lunch.

Shakshuka is from North Africa, but it's popular in the Middle East, too. It has tomatoes, peppers, onions, garlic, and lots of eggs. People usually eat it with bread, for breakfast, lunch, or dinner.

Grammar

Countable and uncountable nouns

1 Complete the table with these words.

| milk | onion | cup | egg | fruit |
| cookie | cheese | rice | sugar | teaspoon |

countable	uncountable
cookie	cheese

2 Read the ingredients for each dish. Correct the three mistakes with uncountable nouns.

Fried rice	Cheesy noodles	Spicy salsa
oils	cheese	tomatoes
rice	garlics	lime
eggs	milk	chillies
vegetables	noodles	salts

oil _____ _____ _____

3 Choose the correct options to complete the conversations.

1 A: Are these the ingredients for ¹cookie / cookies?

   B: No, they're ingredients for ²bread / breads.

2 A: The fruit ³doesn't / don't taste sweet.

   B: Put a little ⁴sugar / sugars on top.

3 A: We need ⁵a / some cheese from the store.

   B: Let's get ⁶a / some rice, too.

4 A: I love ⁷peanut / peanuts.

   B: Me, too. But I don't like them with ⁸salt / salts.

Pronunciation

Understanding *of*

1 🔊 6.1 Listen and match (1–5) with (a–e).

1 a slice of ___e___   a salt

2 a cup of _____   b rice

3 a lot of _____   c chocolate

4 a teaspoon of _____   d tea

5 a bar of _____   e bread

Vocabulary

Places for groceries

1 Complete the sentences with these words.

| convenience store | market | supermarket |

1 I love shopping outside in the summer at the farmer's _____. I like seeing all the fruit and vegetables.

2 I love shopping at the _____ near my house. It's small, but it has all the things I need.

3 I always get bread, cheese, and cookies at the _____. It's very big! I usually drive there. I go there twice a month.

2 Where do you go to buy these things? Why? Write complete sentences that are true for you.

1 cheese and bread: *I always get cheese and bread at the supermarket. It's very big and it is near my house.*

2 fruit and vegetables: _____

_____

3 eggs, rice, noodles: _____

_____

Listening

Look at the Learning to Learn box. Then do the task.

LEARNING TO LEARN: LISTENING

Predicting vocabulary

When you know the topic for a listening activity, think about words linked to the topic. What do you know about the topic? What are some possible words in the audio? It's useful to predict words and then listen for them.

The topic of the listening activity below is food waste. Look at the words in Exercise 1. Which words do you think you will hear in audio track 6.2?

1 🎧 6.2 Listen to a talk about food waste. Circle the words you hear.

book	phone	teacher	train
throw away	groceries	supermarket	restaurant

2 🎧 6.2 Listen again. Complete the notes.

1 People put about _____30_____ % of the food they buy in the trash.

2 People without shopping _____ often buy more groceries.

3 More food goes _____ when people keep it longer.

4 _____ throw away food people don't eat.

Grammar

How much and *how many*

1 Circle the correct options to complete the conversations.

1 A: How *much / many* oil do we use?

  B: We use two bottles of oil.

2 A: How *much / many* teaspoons of sugar do you want?

  B: Two teaspoons, please.

2 Choose the correct options to complete the conversation between a customer and a store clerk.

Slices of cake in a bakery.

A: Excuse me.

B: Yes. Can I help you?

A: I'd like some ¹*cookies / cookie*, please.

B: How ²*many / much* cookies would you like?

A: Just three. And I'd like some ³*bread / breads*, please.

B: Sure. Anything else?

A: I'd like some of that ⁴*cake / cakes*, please. It looks delicious! How ⁵*many / much* sugar is in it?

B: Hmm ... Not ⁶*much / many*. It's not very sweet.

A: OK. Then I'd like three slices, please.

B: Would you like to try our famous ice cream sandwich?

A: How ⁷*many / much* ice cream is in it?

B: A lot!

Pronunciation

Understanding the /h/ sound

1 Listen to these words. Do you hear an /h/ sound? Circle *yes* or *no*.

1 hello   yes   no

2 help   yes   no

3 have   yes   no

4 how much   yes   no

5 how many   yes   no

Writing

1 Read Hassan's blog post below. Write the words *Taste*, *Price*, *Service*, and *Location* in the correct places.

2 Read again. Which word best describes each thing?

1 **Taste:**   (delicious)   OK   poor

2 **Price:**   great   alright   terrible

3 **Service:**   good   average   horrible

4 **Location:** excellent   fine   bad

HASSAN'S FOOD BLOG

Freddie's American Diner
★★★★☆

Freddie's American Diner is a new restaurant on West Street. It opens at 11:30 a.m. for lunch, and it closes at 10 p.m.

1 _____*Taste*_____:

The food is delicious. Their burgers are amazing and their salads are great, too.

2 _____:

The restaurant is very far from downtown. It's very difficult to get there.

3 _____:

The waiters are OK. They're nice, but they're a little slow. Go before 12:00. They're very busy at lunchtime.

4 _____:

The food is very cheap. It's great for students! A cheeseburger is only $4.00.

Freddie's American Diner is a great restaurant, and it isn't expensive. Their burgers are delicious, and their other dishes are great, too.

3 How does Hassan feel about Freddie's American Diner?

   a He loves it.

   b He thinks it's OK.

   c He doesn't like it.

4 Your experience at Freddie's American Diner is very different from Hassan's. What's good, what's just OK, and what's bad? Make notes below.

Main ideas	Details
The food is ___OK.___	*The food is not delicious.* *Their burgers are alright.*
The restaurant is _____	
The waiters are _____	
The price is _____	

5 Write a review of Freddie's American Diner. Write 50–60 words.

- Include a short introduction.
- Write a paragraph for each of your main ideas in Exercise 4.
- Write a conclusion.
- Give the restaurant a star rating.

6 Check your review. Use the checklist.

  ☐ Are the spelling and punctuation correct?

  ☐ Are the grammar and vocabulary correct?

  ☐ Does your review include all the information from the notes in Exercise 5?

Look at the Learning to Learn box. Then do the task.

LEARNING TO LEARN: CHECKING YOUR PROGRESS

It's good to check your progress. Look back at Units 1–6. What are you happy with? What vocabulary and grammar is easy for you? What skills are you comfortable with? What are you not happy with? Which areas do you want to practice more?

1 Complete the table.

- Go through Units 1 to 6 of your Student's Book.
- What do you need to practice more? Write one or two language areas for each row.

	Topics to practice more
Vocabulary	
Grammar	
Reading skills	
Writing skills	
Listening skills	
Communication skills	

2 Think about how you can practice the items in your table. Use these tips.

- Look back at the skills in the Student's Book to practice.
- Do the activities again.
- Ask your teacher for help, too.

5&6 Review 3

Vocabulary

1 Complete the social media posts with these verbs.

call	chat	play	read	sing

> **KenshinR**
>
> It's super cold outside! What do you like doing on winter days like this?? 👍 12
> *Comment ...*
>
> **Mm_Kay**
> Usually, I ¹_____ a book, but sometimes, I ²_____ online with my friends.
>
> **JenZ**
> I usually ³_____ my best friend Tanya, and we go out for a nice, warm meal. Or we just ⁴_____ video games online!
>
> **Tanya**
> We love online karaoke! Join us and ⁵_____ some songs. =)

2 Circle the months. Underline the seasons.

Fall	Spring	April	July
January	August	June	May
October	December	Summer	March
September	November	February	Winter

3 Choose the correct option.

1 It's a drink.   rice / coffee / vegetables

2 It's from plants.   eggs / milk / fruit

3 It's from animals.   meat / noodles / tea

4 It's from the ocean.   cheese / fish / bread

Grammar

1 Complete the sentences. Use the *-ing* form of the verbs in parentheses.

1 I love ___*swimming*___ (swim).

2 Do you like _____ (play) tennis?

3 Adam doesn't like _____ (run) in the morning.

4 I don't like _____ (camp) in the winter.

5 Marta loves _____ (cycle) with her friends.

6 Why does he love _____ (do) yoga at night?

2 Choose the correct options to complete the phone conversation.

R: Hello?

J: Hi, Rebecca.

R: Oh, hi, Josh. Where are you?

J: At the market. But I don't have the shopping list! How ¹*much / many* apples do you want?

R: I'd like two or three ²*apple / apples*. And please get five ³*banana / bananas,* too.

J: What about ⁴*vegetable / vegetables*?

R: We have ⁵*onion / onions*. Just look for some nice ⁶*potato / potatoes*.

J: Alright.

R: And please get some ⁷*rice / rices* too.

J: OK. Do you want some ⁸*ice cream / ice creams*?

R: Yes, please!

J: How ⁹*much / many*?

R: Just a little. Chocolate, please!

Reading

1 Read the article. Underline the ingredients in the three snacks. Then answer the questions.

1 Trail mix and s'mores both have _____ .

2 Trail mix and granola bars both have

_____ .

2 Read the article again. Are the sentences true (T) or false (F)?

1 Trail mix is easy to make.   T   F

2 People usually eat s'mores warm.   T   F

3 S'mores and trail mix have nuts.   T   F

4 Granola bars are a type of cheesecake. T   F

OUTDOOR SNACKS

Do you like hiking and camping? These three snacks are great for the outdoors.

Trail mix
Hikers love trail mix. It usually has nuts, fruit, and chocolate in it. It's great for hiking because it gives you lots of energy. People 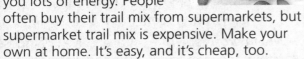 often buy their trail mix from supermarkets, but supermarket trail mix is expensive. Make your own at home. It's easy, and it's cheap, too.

S'mores
The word *s'more* comes from "some more" in "Do you want some more?" And who doesn't want more of this delicious camping favorite? It has only three ingredients: cookies, marshmallows, and chocolate. Cook your s'mores over a fire and eat them warm!

Granola bars
Granola bars are great for hiking. They're a type of cake and they're easy to make. The most important 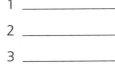 ingredients are oats, butter, and sugar. Many people also put fruit in their granola bars. They're delicious and they're easy to carry around.

Listening

1 🎧 **R3.1** Listen to a radio show. Match the people (1–3) with what they like doing (a–f).

1 Zac   _____ _____

2 Julia   _____ _____

3 Natasha   _____ _____

a camping

b going to the beach

c hiking

d playing video games

e swimming

f eating pizza

2 🎧 **R3.1** Listen again. Choose the correct option.

1 Summer *starts* / *ends* tomorrow.

2 Zac likes camping in the *spring* / *summer*.

3 Julia lives in *Atlanta* / *Jacksonville*.

4 Natasha is an *indoor* / *outdoor* person.

Pronunciation

1 🎧 **R3.2** Listen and match the question beginnings (1–4) with the endings (a–d).

1 What would you   ○   ○ a like to go?

2 Where would you   ○   ○ b like to see?

3 When would you   ○   ○ c like to visit?

4 Who would you   ○   ○ d like to eat?

2 🎧 **R3.3** Listen and write the *-ing* verbs you hear. Listen again and repeat.

1 _____

2 _____

3 _____

4 _____

7 Family and friends

Vocabulary

Family members

1 Read the sentences. Complete the family tree with the correct names.

1 Tomas is Marco's son.

2 Juan is Marco's father.

3 Gabriela is Marco's daughter.

4 Bianca is Gabriela's mother.

5 Ana is Tomas's grandmother.

2 Complete the sentences with these words.

children   husband   parents   sister   wife

1 Matt and Tess have two _____—a son and a daughter.

2 Patricia is married to Jeff. Jeff is her _____.

3 George is married to Aisha. He and his _____ are both 30 years old.

4 Steve's _____ live in Chicago. Steve is their only son.

5 I don't have a brother, but I have a _____. Her name is Saira.

Reading

1 Skim the blog post on page 47. Circle its purpose (a–c). The post describes how Haley and her family …

a like living together.

b don't like living together.

c both like and don't like living together.

2 Read the blog post. Circle the correct answer (a–c).

1 Where do Haley's grandparents live?
   a in the same house as Haley
   b in an apartment next to Haley's house
   c in Haley's living room

2 What percentage of Australians live in a house with grandparents, parents, and children?
   a 6%   b 20%   c 25%

3 What does Haley plan to do next year?
   a go back to school   b get a new job
   c buy a house

3 What do Haley's family like about living together? Check (✓) the reasons Haley talks about.

a ☐ Haley's grandparents like living near their family.

b ☐ Haley's parents can look after her grandparents.

c ☐ Haley can work from home.

d ☐ Haley likes hearing stories from her grandmother.

At home with Haley

In this week's blog post, I want to talk about my home and the people in it. I'm 25 years old, and I live with my brother, my parents, and my grandparents. We live in a large house in the U.K. My grandparents live in the same house. They have their own kitchen, bedroom, bathroom, and living room.

People in some countries often move out of their parents' homes after they finish school or get a job. That is starting to change. A family with grandparents, parents, and children in one house is more common now. Today, 6% of Canadians live with their family like this. In Australia, it's 20%. In the United States, it's 25%.

What do my family like about living together? My grandparents like being near their family. My parents can look after them. And I like hearing stories from my grandmother and learning from her. There's another important reason. I want to buy and move into my own place, but housing prices are very high. Living with my family, I save money. I plan to buy a house next year—I think!

What about you? Do you live with your parents? Do you like living with your parents? Does it work for you? I want to hear what you think!

Grammar

Simple present questions (*Yes / No* questions)

1 Answer the questions about the photo.

Stephen   Jake   Alison

1 Is Jake in the kitchen?
  No, he isn't. _____.

2 Are Stephen and Alison on the couch?
  _____.

3 Is Jake wearing a hat?
  _____.

4 Does Alison have long hair?
  _____.

5 Is the TV off?
  _____.

2 Put the words in order to make questions.

1 have / she / a big family / does
  Does she have a big family _____?

2 mother / is / your / at work
  _____?

3 with his parents / does / live / he
  _____?

4 you / your family history / do / know
  _____?

5 his / are / from Turkey / grandparents
  _____?

3 Complete the conversations with *are, is,* or *does.*

1 A: [1]_____ your sister in college?

  B: Yes, she [2]_____.

  A: [3]_____ she like it?

2 A: [4]_____ your grandmother live with you?

  B: No. She lives in her own apartment downtown.

  A: [5]_____ she like living there?

3 A: [6]_____ your parents home?

  B: My mother [7]_____, but my father is in Spain right now.

Grammar

Simple present questions (open questions)

1 Match the questions (1–6) with the answers (a–f).

1 Where are they?   _d_   a Great!

2 How are you?   _____   b Photos.

3 What are those?   _____   c At 7:45.

4 Who are they?   _____   d At home.

5 Why is she at home?   _____   e My parents.

6 When does it start?   _____   f Because it's cold outside.

2 Correct the mistake in each question.

1 When **do** your class begin?
  *When **does** your class begin?*

2 Who **are** your favorite singer?
  _____

3 Where **do** your grandparents from?
  _____

4 Why **is** she always come to class late?
  _____

5 How **does** you spell your name?
  _____

3 Complete the conversation with *are, is, do,* or *does*.

A: You have a lot of photos on your phone. Who ¹_____ that?

B: Oh, that's my sister Terry.

A: Where ²_____ she live?

B: She lives in Paris.

A: What ³_____ she ⁴_____ there?

B: She works in a hotel.

A: And who ⁵_____ they?

B: That's her husband and two children.

Pronunciation

Saying short and long vowel sounds

1 🎧 7.1 Listen to ten words. Write short vowel (S) or long vowel (L) for each word.

1 h**a**t _S_ h**a**te _L_   4 n**o**te ____ n**o**t ____

2 t**ee**n ____ t**e**n ____   5 c**u**te ____ c**u**t ____

3 b**i**t ____ b**i**te ____

2 🎧 7.1 Listen again and repeat.

Look at the Learning to Learn box. Then do the task.

LEARNING TO LEARN: PRONUNCIATION

Using a mirror to practice pronunciation
It can be helpful to look into a mirror when you pronounce words with similar sounds. Pay attention to your lips, tongue, and the shape of your mouth.

Look into a mirror. Practice saying the ten words in Pronunciation Exercise 1.

Vocabulary

Appearance and personality

1 What do the words (1–10) describe? Write A (appearance) or P (personality).

1 long hair	_A_	6 clever	____
2 nice	____	7 short	____
3 blond hair	____	8 tall	____
4 funny	____	9 interesting	____
5 quiet	____	10 dark hair	____

2 Circle the correct options to complete the text.

Joel and Lacy are my neighbors. Joel is 35 and Lacy is 37. Joel is ¹*tall* / *long* and has ²*quiet* / *dark* hair. He's really ³*short* / *funny*—he always make me laugh! He's also quite ⁴*long* / *clever*. I know he's a teacher. He's a very ⁵*blond* / *interesting* person—not boring at all. I really like talking to him. Lacy has ⁶*blond* / *quiet* hair. It's not very ⁷*tall* / *long*. She likes it ⁸*nice* / *short*. She's a very ⁹*long* / *nice* person. She's kind, but she's a little ¹⁰*interesting* / *quiet* sometimes. She doesn't talk much.

Listening

1 🎧 **7.2** Listen to the podcast. What is its main idea? Circle the correct answer.

   a Appearance is important.

   b Personality is important.

   c Some people are bad friends.

2 🎧 **7.2** Listen again. Complete the sentences.

   1 A good friend is kind to you and to _____.

   2 A good friend _____. They're interested in your life.

   3 A good friend makes you _____.

   4 A good friend is _____ there for you.

   5 A good friend says what's _____.

Look at the Learning to Learn box. Then do the task.

LEARNING TO LEARN: LISTENING

Using audioscripts

Audioscripts are very useful. Don't read them before you do a task. Read them after you finish the task. Look for things that you don't understand.
Here are some tips for reading an audioscript:

- Underline new words.
- Find the meaning of new words in a dictionary.
- Listen to and practice the pronunciation of new words.

🎧 **7.3** Listen to a track from the Student's Book again. Read the script below and practice the tips above.

1 Antonio often makes me laugh. He's funny.
2 Jessica does very well at school. She's clever.
3 Antonio is kind and easy to talk to. He's nice.
4 Jessica has a lot of ideas. She's never boring. She's interesting.
5 Sometimes, Antonio doesn't talk much. He's quiet.

Grammar

Adjectives

1 Circle the correct options to complete the text.

My friend Chirawan lives in Udon Thani, Thailand. She ¹*is / has* tall and ²*is / has* long black hair. She ³*is / has* brown eyes. I love her personality. She ⁴*is / has* funny and nice, and everyone loves being around her. She has a ⁵*nice family / family nice*, too. Her parents are very ⁶*interesting / interestings*.

2 Rewrite the sentences. Use the verb *be*.

   1 I have brown eyes.

      My eyes are brown. _____

   2 She has short hair.

      Her _____.

   3 That's a funny movie.

      That _____.

   4 She has beautiful clothes.

      Her _____.

   5 They have nice friends.

      Their _____.

   6 This is an interesting photo.

      This _____.

Pronunciation

Saying words with "gr"

1 🎧 7.4 Listen. Do the words have "gr"? Circle *yes* or *no*.

1 yes no   3 yes no   5 yes no

2 yes no   4 yes no   6 yes no

2 🎧 7.5 Listen and repeat.

1 group   4 grocery

2 grade   5 kilogram

3 agree   6 grandson

Writing

1 Read the text message. Match the sentences in bold (1–7) with their function (a–f).

> How are things? Do you have time on Saturday morning? **¹I need someone to meet my friend Jake at the train station.** **²I have an exam then.** His train gets in at 9:45. **³He's tall with short blond hair.** **⁴He's 23 years old.** **⁵He's a very interesting and funny person.** I think you will like him. **⁶You both love movies a lot.** **⁷He lives in Los Angeles and wants to be an actor.**

a describes someone's personality _____

b says why you need help _____

c says what the people have in common _____

d describes someone's appearance _____

e says that you need help _____

f gives other information about someone

_____ _____

2 A new student is in the cafeteria. She needs someone to show her around school. Ask your classmate to meet her. Make notes before writing a text message.

- Say you need help.
- Say why you need help.
- Describe the new student.
- Say what the new student and your classmate have in common.
- Give other useful or interesting information.

3 Write a text message to a classmate. Use your notes in Exercise 2 to help you. Write 40–50 words.

4 Check your text message. Use the checklist.

☐ Are the spelling and punctuation correct?

☐ Are the grammar and vocabulary correct?

☐ Does your text message include all the information from the notes in Exercise 2?

Look at the Learning to Learn box. Complete your learning journal.

LEARNING TO LEARN: YOUR LEARNING JOURNAL

Your learning journal is a place to write new vocabulary and grammar. You can use it to check your progress in other areas, too. Writing about your progress is useful, but you can also make audio recordings with your phone or computer. This is good practice for speaking and pronunciation. Follow these steps:

1 Write sentences for your entry.

2 Practice saying the sentences.

3 Record your audio entry.

---

1 Complete the sentences. Think about reading, listening, speaking, and writing.

I feel good about _____.

I need to review _____.

I want to practice _____ *more.*

2 Record your audio entry. Use your sentences in Task 1 to help you.

8 Things we can do

Vocabulary

Common abilities

1 Circle the correct verb to complete the phrases.

1 (ride) / play / drive a bike

2 talk / speak / say a language

3 write / make / paint a picture

4 go / climb / walk a mountain

5 cook / do / take a meal

6 do / bake / cook a cake

2 Label the photos with the phrases from Exercise 1.

1 _____

4 _____

2 _____

5 _____

3 _____ride a bike_____

6 _____

Reading

1 Read the article. What is it mainly about? Circle the correct answer.

a why robot suits are expensive

b how robot suits help workers

2 Scan the article on page 53 for these words. Match them to the correct pictures.

a robot b suit c factory d electricity e lift

1 __d__ 2 ____ 3 ____ 4 ____ 5 ____

3 Find these pronouns in the text. Circle what they refer to.

1 *it*   a the worker   b the job

2 *they*   a robot suits   b people

3 *them*   a the users   b the robot suits

Look at the Learning to Learn box. Then do the task.

LEARNING TO LEARN: READING

Filling in gaps

A text doesn't always tell the reader everything. Sometimes the reader needs to fill in the gaps. Readers can use what they already know about the topic, or what they think about it. As you read, ask yourself questions like *How?* and *Why?*

Look at the article on page 53. Can you answer these questions? Make notes.

1 How can the suits help firefighters?

2 What other jobs can the suits be useful for?

A worker wearing a robot suit

Robot suits

Can you lift 20 kilograms? How about 40 kilograms? Now imagine doing that non-stop, for hours and hours every day. This is the job of many workers around the world, and **it** isn't easy. What can we do to help these workers? One solution is a robot suit that you can wear.

Suits like these look like they're from movies or comic books, but **they** are real. In some countries, nurses, firefighters, and factory workers already use them. These strong metal suits use electricity to help people pick up and move heavy things. They make many difficult jobs easy.

But how much do suits like these help? Many people can lift about 30 to 40 kilograms. With robot suits, they can lift more than 100 kilograms. And that's not all. The suits do almost all the work for **them**. They help workers carry a lot more things for many more hours.

Suits like these are expensive, but there are some benefits for businesses. Over time, these robot suits save them money and they help keep their workers safe.

Grammar

Can and *can't*

1 Correct the mistake in each sentence or question.

1 She **cant** answer the question.

*She **can't** answer the question.*

2 Can he **bakes** a cake?

_____

3 Can your friends **playing** soccer?

_____

4 He can **speaking** Russian.

_____

5 Can **run** you five kilometers?

_____

2 Rewrite each sentence using *can* or *can't*.

1 William is good at playing tennis.

William can play tennis.

2 Cal doesn't know how to speak French.

_____

3 Patricia is really bad at singing.

_____

4 Brynn knows how to fix a computer.

_____

5 Sachiko plays the violin very well.

_____

6 Ricardo doesn't know how to swim.

_____

3 Can you do these things? Write true sentences.

1 play the guitar

I can play the guitar.

2 drive a car

_____

3 speak Spanish

_____

4 ride a bike

_____

Look at the Learning to Learn box. Then do the task.

LEARNING TO LEARN: GRAMMAR

Remembering grammar rules

When you learn new grammar, it can be useful to write example sentences and questions with the grammar. This can help you to remember it. Try to write a positive sentence, a negative sentence, a *Yes / No* question, and an open question.

Positive: *He works in an office.*
Negative: *He doesn't work in an office.*
Yes / No question: *Does he work in an office?*
Open question: *Where does he work?*

Look at the examples above. Write sentences and questions using your own ideas.

Positive: _____ .

Negative: _____ .

Yes / No question: _____ ?

Open question: _____ ?

Pronunciation

Stressing *can't*

1 🎧 8.1 Listen and circle the correct options.

1 He *can / can't* cook.

2 They *can / can't* swim.

3 She *can / can't* ride a bike.

4 We *can / can't* run a marathon.

5 I *can / can't* play the piano.

6 He *can / can't* stand on his head.

2 🎧 8.1 Listen again and repeat.

Vocabulary

Adjectives for animals

1 Look at the photos. Circle the two adjectives that describe each animal.

1 slow   heavy   small

2 strong   small   large

3 large   light   beautiful

4 slow   fast   small

2 Circle the correct option to complete each sentence.

1 Tortoises are very *slow / strong*. They don't walk fast at all.

2 Bears are *beautiful / strong*. Some can lift over 500 kilograms.

3 Hummingbirds are *light / slow*. They weigh between 2.5 and 4.5 grams.

4 Rabbits have *large / fast* ears, so they can hear things far away.

5 Elephants are very *fast / heavy*. Some weigh about 6,000 kilograms!

Listening

1 🎧 8.2 Listen to a talk about animals at a wildlife park in Australia. Circle the animals (a–c) the guide talks about.

a lions, cheetahs, and pandas

b elephants, tortoises, and rabbits

c kangaroos, koalas, and camels

2 🎧 8.2 Listen to the talk again. Check (✓) the things that are true.

1 Kangaroos …
☐ are from Australia.
☐ can swim.
☐ can walk backwards.

2 Koalas …
☐ are a type of bear.
☐ sleep a lot.
☐ are sometimes dangerous.

3 Camels …
☐ are from Australia.
☐ can run fast.
☐ can drink a lot of water.

A sloth

Grammar

and, or, but, because

1 Circle the correct option (a or b) to complete each sentence.

1 Pablo can cook and _____.

  a he can bake
  b he doesn't enjoy it.

2 Sara loves playing soccer, but _____.

  a she likes playing tennis
  b she's not very good at it

3 I can't lift the box because _____.

  a it's very heavy
  b I can lift the chair

4 We can see the black bears now, or _____.

  a we can see the pandas
  b they're cute and friendly

2 Match the sentence beginnings (1–4) with the endings (a–d).

1 Elephants are big and _____ a it is very fast.

2 The rabbit is small, but _____ b Tuesday.

3 I want to work here _____ c strong.
  because

4 I can come on   _____ d I'm good with
  Monday or   computers.

3 Circle the correct options to complete the text.

Sloths are amazing animals, ¹*and /but/ because* it's not easy to see them. They sleep 15 hours a day. They usually sleep high up in the trees ²*but / or / because* it's a safe place for them. They are very slow walkers, ³*but / or / because* they are strong swimmers. They love being in the water ⁴*and / but / or* they can stay underwater for 40 minutes. Sloths live in Central and South America, ⁵*but / or / because* you can find them in many zoos.

Pronunciation

Saying the letter "g"

1 🔊 8.3 Listen and check (✓) the sound you hear.

	/g/ (go)	/dʒ/ (age)	/ŋ/ (sing)
1		✓	
2			
3			
4			
5			
6			

2 🔊 8.3 Listen again and repeat.

Writing

1 Match the sentences from application forms (a–h) with the tips for applying for a job (1–4).

a I'm a hard worker.

b I can speak English.

c I can't speak Italian well.

d I want to work for you because …

e I'm not good at using a computer.

f I always do a great job.

g I'm good at cooking burgers.

h I would like to work here because …

1 Say why you want the job.   _____ _____

2 Say what you can do.   _____ _____

3 Don't say what you can't do.   _____ _____

4 Say what you are like as a person. _____ _____

2 Choose one of the jobs below to apply for. Make notes about:

- which job you want and why you want it
- what skills are important for the job
- what you can do
- what you are like as a person

Jobs

tour guide   receptionist   baker
math teacher   party planner   waiter

3 Complete the extra information field of a job application. Write 40–50 words. Remember:

- Say what you can do
- Don't say what you can't do.

4 Check your application. Use the checklist.

☐ Are the spelling and punctuation correct?

☐ Are the grammar and vocabulary correct?

☐ Does your application include the information from your notes in Exercise 2?

Look at the Learning to Learn box. Then do the task.

LEARNING TO LEARN: MAKING GROUP PLANS

It's important to use English outside of the classroom. One option is to meet your classmates and speak English with them. You can have fun and practice your English at the same time. Here are some ideas for things you can do:

- Agree to read the same news article and then meet to discuss it.
- Go to the movie theater together and discuss the movie later.
- Go out for lunch and talk about different foods you like.
- Agree to watch the same TV show and then meet to discuss it.
- Bring a favorite thing or photo and discuss it.

Make plans to meet your classmates. Choose one of the activities above or think of your own.

7&8 Review 4

Vocabulary

1 Look at the puzzle. Find and circle eight family words.

```
W  B  B  R  O  T  H  E  R  W  M  B
I  D  A  U  G  H  T  E  R  Z  L  H
F  S  O  N  O  W  M  O  T  H  E  R
E  Y  H  C  I  H  U  S  B  A  N  D
C  E  F  A  T  H  E  R  R  S  B  Y
S  H  E  F  P  S  I  S  T  E  R  I
```

2 Circle the correct option to complete each sentence.

1 My sister's hair is very *long / short*. She wants to cut it.

2 Our teacher is *interesting / quiet*. She always tells us amazing stories.

3 Farah is very *funny / clever*. She always gets good grades.

4 My brother is on the school basketball team. He's very *long / tall*.

5 Nicole is a *quiet / nice* person. She doesn't talk much.

3 Complete the phrases with the correct verbs.

1 _b_ _a_ _k_ _e_ a cake

2 __ __ __ __ __ a car

3 __ __ __ __ __ a musical instrument

4 __ __ __ __ __ a bike

5 __ __ __ __ __ a language

6 __ __ __ __ __ a picture

4 Circle the correct options to complete each conversation.

1 A: The butterfly is really [1]*heavy / beautiful*.

   B: It is very [2]*small / slow*, too. It's smaller than my hand!

2 A: Cheetahs are [3]*strong / small* animals.

   B: And they're [4]*slow / fast*, too. They can run faster than a car.

3 A: Rabbits are [5]*heavy / small* animals.

   B: But they can run really [6]*fast / large*!

Grammar

1 Put the words in order to make questions.

1 her / what / is / last name / ?
   What is her last name?

2 like / does / she / swimming / ?
   _____

3 he / is / teacher / interesting / an / ?
   _____

4 do / grandparents / where / your / live / ?
   _____

5 spell / do / your name / you / how / ?
   _____

6 parents / are / your / from / the U.K. / ?
   _____

2 Circle the correct options to complete the text.

My best friend is Layla. She's really nice [1]*and / or* she loves helping people. People like being around her [2]*but / because* she's funny, too. She often tells stories about her life. They're usually about her family, [3]*but / because* sometimes they're about her job. I love talking to Layla. We often just meet at a restaurant for lunch [4]*and / or* dinner and talk for hours!

Reading

1 Look at the photo. What is the article about? Circle the correct answer.

   a a father and son music group

   b an online musical instrument store

   c a person who plays many instruments

2 Read the article again. Answer the questions.

   1 Where does Neil live?

   _____

   2 How many instruments can he play?

   _____

   3 Which instruments do his parents play?

   _____

   4 How many hours does Neil practice every day?

   _____

   5 What does he want to learn?

   _____

Some musicians can play two, three, or even four musical instruments. But one teenager in California can play 107! Neil Nayyar has instruments from Italy, China, India, and many other countries, and he can play them all.

Nobody knows where Neil gets his musical abilities from. His parents can't play any instruments, and he doesn't have brothers or sisters to learn from. For some reason, Neil is just good at music. But it's not just luck. Neil practices a lot too—about six to eight hours a day! He has 78 music teachers from around the world. He can't visit them all, so he learns from them online.

Neil loves music, but he has many other interests, too. He can paint and he's good at martial arts. He loves dancing, and he wants to learn singing and acting. So what's next for Neil? It's musical instrument number 108, of course!

Listening

1 🎧 **R4.1** Listen to the advertisement from Star Studios. What is it for? Circle the correct answer.

   a people who want to make movies

   b people who want to act in movies

2 🎧 **R4.1** Listen again. Are the sentences true (T) or false (F)?

   1 The program is for two months.   T F

   2 There are all kinds of jobs.   T F

   3 People work on real movie sets.   T F

   4 People can work with writers,   T F
      directors, and actors.

   5 People need to go to the studio to   T F
      complete a form.

Pronunciation

1 🎧 **R4.2** Listen. Are the vowel sounds in the two words the same or different? Write same (S) or different (D).

   1 man   hat _____

   2 bed   when _____

   3 him   wife _____

   4 not   goes _____

   5 but   run   _____

2 🎧 **R4.3** Listen and complete the sentences with *can* or *can't*.

   1 Hal _____ play the piano well.

   2 Kaley _____ count to ten in five languages.

   3 Dmitri _____ fix your computer.

   4 Shweta _____ swim.

   5 David _____ sing, but he _____ dance.

Travel

Vocabulary

Different ways to travel

1 Circle the correct verb for each type of transportation.

1 drive /
fly

3 take /
sail

5 sail /
take

7 fly /
take

2 fly /
sail

4 drive /
ride

6 drive /
fly

8 ride /
drive

2 Complete the text. Use words from Exercise 1.

I love exploring Bangkok, Thailand. When I'm there, I usually ¹_____ a motorcycle around the city. But you can also just ²_____ a taxi. To save money, ³_____ a train. There are many stations and you get a great view of the city. Or ⁴_____ down the river by boat. You can visit many famous tourist sites this way. Finally, ⁵_____ a *tuk tuk* (a three-wheeled open vehicle). They're a fun, cheap way to travel in the evening, when it's cool.

A *tuk tuk* on the road

Reading

1 Look at the photos and skim paragraph 1 on page 61. Circle the meaning of "glamping."

a camping in a small tent

b a comfortable camping experience

c camping alone with no other people around

2 Read the article. Where does the article say you can do these things? Check (✓) the places.

	Merzouga	Juluchuca	Wicklow Hills
drive around			
go online for free			
have a campfire			
enjoy music			
visit a beach			
see wildlife			

3 Read the text again. Answer the questions.

1 What is "couscous"?

_____

2 What can you see from a treehouse in Juluchuca?

_____

3 What is a yurt?

_____

4 What wildlife can you see in Wicklow Hills?

_____

Let's go glamping!

Camping is great, but it's not for everyone. Some people don't like carrying a heavy bag or sleeping in a small tent. For these people, there's glamping. Glamping (_glamorous_ + _camping_) is camping in an easy and comfortable way. Here are three places to go glamping.

Merzouga, MOROCCO

Spend a few quiet nights in a beautiful tent in the Sahara Desert. Enjoy delicious seven-vegetable couscous (a famous Moroccan dish) in the restaurant tent. Ride a camel or drive around the desert during the day. At night, sit around the fire and listen to Moroccan music.

◄ Tents in Merzouga, Morocco

Juluchuca, MEXICO

Enjoy a view of the ocean from a beautiful treehouse that is two meters in the air. These treehouses have everything you need for a comfortable stay: a large bed, a bathroom, Wi-Fi, and more. There's a beautiful beach, too.

A treehouse ► in Juluchuca, Mexico

Wicklow Hills, IRELAND

Stay in a yurt (a Mongolian tent) on an Irish farm. There's a bed inside each yurt and a place to have a fire outside. Explore Ireland's green hills, and watch birds and other animals. (Wicklow Hills is a great place for bird watching). Finally, you can enjoy delicious meals in an old farmhouse.

▲ A yurt

Warsaw, Poland

Grammar

There is and *There are*

1 Complete the sentences and question with *is* or *are*.

1 There _____ many old buildings in my city.

2 There _____ a pretty beach.

3 There _____ many outdoor markets.

4 There _____ a beautiful park.

5 _____ there an art museum?

2 Put the words in order to make sentences or questions.

1 train station / is / new / there / a

   There is a new train station _____.

2 two / there / are / museums

   _____.

3 is / university / there / a

   _____?

4 any / there / aren't / Mexican restaurants

   _____.

5 information center / there / an / is

   _____?

3 Circle the correct options to complete the conversation.

A: So, you're from Warsaw. What can you do there?

B: Well, [1]*there's / there are* many interesting things. People come to see the old town square, of course.

A: Are there any famous museums?

B: Yes. There are [2]*some / any* wonderful museums in the city. The National Museum is excellent.

A: [3]*Is / Are* there an outdoor market?

B: Yes, there [4]*is / are*. There are [5]*some / any* amazing restaurants, too. Polish food is delicious!

A: What about hiking? Are there [6]*a / any* mountains?

B: No, there [7]*isn't / aren't*. But there [8]*is / are* many places to walk in the city.

Vocabulary

The weather

1 Write the weather word under the pictures.

a _____   b _____   c _____   d _____

2 Choose the correct options to complete the descriptions.

Spring in Seoul, South Korea is great. The days are warm and dry. You don't usually need an umbrella because there isn't much ¹*rain / wind*.

Many people visit Istanbul, Turkey in the summer. It's sometimes hot because the ²*sun / snow* is out all day, but the ³*wind / sun* helps keep you cool.

Fall days in Montevideo, Uruguay are usually warm. But it can get really ⁴*dry / wet* when the rain falls.

Winter in Reykjavik, Iceland is cold but beautiful. Sometimes, the ⁵*wind / snow* falls, but it doesn't usually stay on the ground long.

Look at the Learning to Learn box. Then do the task.

LEARNING TO LEARN: VOCABULARY

Using flashcards

When you learn new words, make flashcards to help you remember them. Write the new word on one side of a card. Draw a picture on the other side. You can use different color cards for different types of words. For example, use yellow cards for nouns, blue cards for verbs, and white cards for adjectives.

Make flashcards for new words in this unit or a previous unit. Then try these tips to help you remember the new words.

1 Look at the picture, try to remember the word, then check.

2 Think of and say a sentence with each new word.

3 Take out the words that are easy to remember.

4 Check through the cards again.

5 After a few days, repeat the steps until you can remember all the words.

Listening

1 🎧 9.1 Listen to three advertisements. Match the parks (1–3) with the countries (a–c).

1 Chitwan National Park   _____   a Colombia

2 Samaria National Park   _____   b Nepal

3 Tayrona National Park   _____   c Greece

2 🎧 **9.1** Listen again. What do the advertisements say? Circle the correct options.

Advertisement 1

1 *Drive / Walk* around the park or travel by boat.

2 *Come / Don't come* between October and March.

Advertisement 2

3 Enjoy the views and then *play / swim* in the ocean.

4 *Hike / Don't hike* between May and October.

Advertisement 3

5 *Relax / Swim* and enjoy the warm sun.

6 *Visit / Don't visit* the park in February.

Grammar

Object pronouns

1 Complete the sentences with these words.

him	her	it	me	them	us	you

1 This ticket is for my father. Please give _____ to _____.

2 My friends are in your class. Say "hello" to _____ for _____.

3 Where are Tran and Wei Ting? Can you help _____ find _____?

4 Phoebe needs to talk to her brother. Tell _____ to call _____.

5 This is Matthew's umbrella. Can you please give _____ to _____?

2 Put the words in order to make sentences.

1 me / it / give / to

Give it to me .

2 him / help / they / can't

_____.

3 it / to / wants / he / use

_____.

4 to see / I / you / want

_____.

5 us / they / traveling / like / with

_____.

Look at the Learning to Learn box. Then do the tasks.

LEARNING TO LEARN: GRAMMAR

Using a grammar checker

Grammar checkers can be useful. Many computers have them, and you can find many online. Grammar checkers show many of the grammar and spelling errors in a text. They also tell you how to correct them. However, grammar checkers aren't perfect. They don't find every error, and they sometimes make mistakes, too. Use grammar checkers to help you, but always read and check your own work, as well.

1 Put this text into a grammar checker.

Spring is great time visit Croatia. We at Coast Travel have tours to beaches, mountains, and beautiful villages. There is sometimes rains, but visitors can to expect warm days with lots of sun.

2 Answer these questions.

1 What errors does the grammar checker find?

2 How often would you use a grammar checker?

Pronunciation

Saying /w/ and /v/

1 🎧 **9.2** Listen to six words. What sound does each word begin with? Write *w* or *v*.

1 very ____   3 way ____   5 view ____

2 wet ____   4 van ____   6 why ____

2 🎧 **9.2** Listen again and repeat.

Pronunciation

Saying /θ/

1 🔊 **9.3** Listen and circle the numbers you hear.

1 the *ninth / nineteenth* of January

2 the *fifth / fifteenth* of March

3 the *twentieth / seventh* of April

4 the *eleventh / tenth* of October

2 🔊 **9.3** Listen again and repeat.

Writing

1 Complete the sentences with these words.

place	are	vacation	love
amazing	things	weather	

1 I'm on _____ in Dubai.

2 It's _____!

3 I _____ it here!

4 The cool _____ is perfect.

5 There _____ some excellent stores.

6 There are so many _____ to do.

7 It's a great _____ to relax.

2 Circle the reason (a or b) for using an exclamation mark (!).

1 This beach is perfect!

 a The writer is happy.
 b The writer is angry.

2 Please don't forget your passport!

 a The writer is surprised.
 b Something is important.

3 The weather is terrible!

 a The writer is happy.
 b The writer is angry.

4 Oh, wow. You're here!

 a The writer is surprised.
 b Something is important.

3 Imagine you are on vacation. Answer these questions. Make notes.

1 Where are you?

2 How is the weather?

3 What is the place like?

4 What can you find there?

5 What can you do there?

4 Write a postcard. Use your notes from Exercise 3. Write 45–50 words.

5 Check your postcard. Use the checklist.

☐ Are the spelling and punctuation correct?

☐ Are the grammar and vocabulary correct?

☐ Does your postcard include all the information from the notes in Exercise 3?

Look at the Learning to Learn box. Complete your learning journal.

LEARNING TO LEARN: YOUR LEARNING JOURNAL

Your learning journal is a great place to record your progress. You can write in your journal or make an audio entry. Or you can make a video entry with your phone, tablet, or computer. This is good practice for speaking and pronunciation. Follow these steps:

1 Write down what you want to say for your journal entry.

2 Practice saying the sentences.

3 Record your video entry.

1 Complete the sentences. How do you feel about Unit 9? Think about reading, listening, speaking and writing.

I feel good about my _____.

I need to review _____.

I want to practice _____ *more.*

2 Record your video entry. Use the sentences in Task 1 and add your own sentences, too.

10 Staying healthy

Vocabulary

Body parts

1 Read the clues. Complete the crossword with parts of the body.

Across

3 This is between your eyes and mouth.

4 Your hand is at the end of this.

7 You put shoes on these.

9 This can be dark or blond.

10 This helps you stand or walk.

Down

1 You write with this.

2 You wear a hat on this.

5 You open this to talk.

6 You listen with this.

8 You see with this.

2 Circle the correct part of the body

1 arm /
ear

3 foot /
mouth

5 leg /
hair

2 hand /
head

4 nose /
eye

6 ear /
mouth

Reading

1 Skim the discussion board on page 67. Write the correct headings in spaces A–C.

| Move! | Picture it | Keep things neat |

2 Read the discussion board again. Circle the correct option (a or b).

1 Does danni54 think a little stress is OK?

  a Yes.   b No.

2 What makes rvasquez3 stressed?

  a being a nurse b putting things away

3 How long do you hold your breath with the 4-7-8 technique?

  a 4 seconds   b 7 seconds

3 Match these sentences (a–d) to the correct spaces (1–4) on the discussion board.

a Any type of music is fine.

b Exercise a little every day.

c There's a cool wind in the air.

d I throw them away.

What do you do to reduce stress?

@danni54

What do you do to reduce your stress?

A little stress is OK—it can even be good for you. But I have a lot of stress right now. I go to university and I have a job. It sometimes feels like too much. What do you do to lower your stress?

 You and 2 others   Seen by 9

👍 Like   💬 Comment

Write a comment …

@rvasquez3

A: _____

I'm a nurse, so I have a lot of stress, too. For me, coming home to a clean apartment is very important. It helps me feel relaxed. I always put things away. And I don't keep things I don't need. ¹_____ Here's a pic!

@umberto55

Listen to music

Music is great for stress. I listen to music all the time: when I wake up in the morning, when I travel to university, when I study, or before I go to sleep. ²_____

@CarrieAnne

B: _____

Exercise helps me lower my stress. So does being outside in a nice, quiet park. Visit a park or go for a hike. Or just go out for a walk or a run and enjoy the fresh air. ³_____

@pinkie

Breathe …

Try the 4-7-8 breathing exercise. Find a quiet place. Breathe in with your nose for four seconds. Hold your breath for seven seconds. Finally, breathe out with your mouth for eight seconds. Do this a few times. It works for me!

@winstonK

C: _____

Here's an idea. Close your eyes and think of a nice place, like a beautiful beach. It's a quiet day and the weather is perfect. ⁴_____ The sun is out and the sand feels warm under your feet. Relax and take a journey to your own special place.

Look at the Learning to Learn box. Then do the tasks. Look at page 67 for the discussion board.

Look at page 67 for the discussion board.

LEARNING TO LEARN: READING

Making notes about a text

When you read a text, it can be useful to make notes on the important information. Try these tips for making notes:

- Find the main ideas or important details.
- Use your own words to describe things.
- Use letters or short words to save time, e.g., "V" or "vocab" for "vocabulary."

1 Look at these notes from the "Breathe ..." section of the discussion board. What information does the reader think is important? Do you agree?

Breathe
4-7-8 ex
breathe in (nose) = 4 secs
hold = 7 secs
breathe out (mouth) = 8 secs

2 Make notes on the other sections of the discussion board.

Grammar

Present continuous

1 Write the *-ing* form of each verb.

1 buy *buying*   5 write _____

2 work _____   6 run _____

3 use _____   7 play _____

4 shop _____   8 swim _____

2 Change the verbs in bold to the *-ing* form.

1 Todd is **look** at a soccer shirt.

 Todd is looking at a soccer shirt.

2 Where are your parents **stay**?

 _____?

3 Nancy and Leo are **buy** train tickets.

 _____.

4 What are you **watch** on TV?

 _____?

5 Who is Dana **play** tennis with?

 _____?

3 Complete the conversations with these words.

doing	starting	studying
talking	waiting	watching

1 A: Kym and I are ¹_____ for you.

 B: Sorry, we're on the bus.

 A: Try to hurry. The concert is ²_____ right now.

2 A: What are you and Kerry ³_____?

 B: We're ⁴_____ a video online.

 A: Do you want to come over?

3 A: Mario isn't ⁵_____ now.

 B: Why not?

 A: I'm not sure. I think he's ⁶_____ to his friends.

Look at the Learning to Learn box. Then do the task.

LEARNING TO LEARN: GRAMMAR

Texting and chatting online

One way to practice grammar is to use it texting or chatting online. This is also good for your vocabulary, spelling, and punctuation.

Form a chat group with some of your classmates. Use the present continuous to ask questions. For example:

Are you studying?

What are you doing now?

Runners in the Amsterdam Marathon

Pronunciation

Understanding word groups

1 🔊 **10.1** **Listen and underline the three stressed words in each sentence.**

1 She's <u>riding</u> her <u>bike</u> in the <u>park</u>.

2 We're watching a movie on TV.

3 He's training for a marathon with his friend.

4 I'm buying some bananas in the market.

Vocabulary

Exercise and training

1 **Complete the sentences with these words.**

exercise	learn	practice	prepare

1 Keysha wants to _____ how to play the guitar. She needs a teacher.

2 Malik and Xavier _____ a lot. They want to be healthy.

3 My friend and I often _____ our English with new people we meet.

4 I need to _____ for my exam. I really want to get a good grade.

2 **Circle the correct option to complete each sentence.**

1 I am going to the gym to *prepare / exercise*.

2 Caleb wants to *learn / prepare* how to ride a bike.

3 Ellie is *preparing / learning* for her chess match now.

4 Iva wants to *practice / exercise* singing today.

3 **Answer these questions. Write complete sentences.**

1 Who do you practice your English with?

_____

2 What do you do to prepare for an exam?

_____

Listening

1 ⟨🔊 10.2⟩ **Listen to a workshop. What is it about? Circle the correct answer.**

a staying healthy while traveling

b exercises you can do at work

c exercises you can do with your friends

2 ⟨🔊 10.2⟩ **Listen again. Number the exercises (a–c) in the order the speakers describe them.**

a ____

b ____

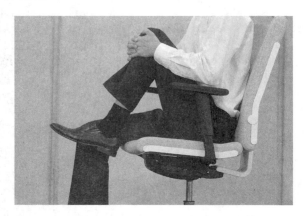

c ____

3 ⟨🔊 10.2⟩ **Listen again. Answer the questions.**

1 What does the man use to remember to exercise?

_____

2 What part of the body is the second exercise good for?

_____

3 Does the man lift his right knee or left knee first?

_____

Grammar
Present continuous vs. simple present

1 Circle the correct option to complete each sentence.

1 Sometimes, Val *goes* / *is going* camping in the summer.

2 George *plays* / *is playing* tennis right now.

3 I *don't exercise* / *am not exercising* very often.

4 Right now, we *learn* / *are learning* how to speak Italian.

5 *Does she watch* / *Is she watching* sports every weekend?

6 Celia *prepares* / *is preparing* for her exams right now.

2 Complete the text. Use the simple present or present continuous form of the verb in parentheses.

Eleanor ¹___*exercises*___ (exercise) every day. She ²_____ (run) a lot, but she knows good health is not just about exercising. She eats healthy food, too. Right now, Eleanor ³_____ (train) for a marathon. Usually, she ⁴_____ (eat) three meals a day, but these days, she ⁵_____ (try) something new. She ⁶_____ (eat) five small meals a day. She has more energy to train this way.

Pronunciation

Understanding intonation in directions

1 🔊 **10.3** **Listen. When does the intonation go down? Circle the correct words in bold.**

1 Go **left** and then **walk straight**.

2 Go **straight**, turn right **at the bank**, and walk straight **to the market**.

3 Turn left at **the high school**, walk for **100 meters**, and **turn right**.

4 Drive to **the park**, turn left at **the lake**, and continue for **two kilometers**.

Writing

1 **Look at these survey results. What do they show? Circle the correct option to complete the sentence.**

Right now, town people are buying *more* / *less* fruit every week. The fruit at the new supermarket is expensive. Only the strawberries are cheap.

Our Town		
Kilograms of fruit people buy every week		
	Usually	**Now**
Apples	182	94
Oranges	169	77
Bananas	129	61
Strawberries	101	134

2 **Look at the survey results again. Make notes for a report about them. Use your own ideas.**

1 What changes do you see?

2 Why are these changes happening?

3 Are any of the numbers interesting or unusual?

4 Is there a problem? How can you fix it?

3 **Look at your notes in Exercise 2. Think about how you want to start your report.**

1 What is a good title for your report?

2 What is the reason for your report?

4 **Write a report to explain the survey results. Use your notes in Exercises 2 and 3. Write 50–75 words.**

5 **Check your report. Use the checklist.**

☐ Are the spelling and punctuation correct?

☐ Are the grammar and vocabulary correct?

☐ Does your report include all your information from Exercises 2 and 3?

Look at the Learning to Learn box. Then do the tasks.

LEARNING TO LEARN: GOOD LEARNING ROUTINES

Learning a new language can sometimes be difficult. Good habits make learning easier. Try to make them a part of your daily routine.

1 **Read these habits of a good learner. Which are true for you?**

1 I write in my learning journal often.

2 I ask questions in class.

3 I take regular breaks.

4 I practice English outside of class.

5 I often review my lessons and notes.

6 I think about what I do well.

7 I think about areas I can improve.

2 **Look at your answers in Task 1. Answer the questions.**

1 What habits don't you have?

2 Do you think those habits are useful?

3 Do you have other good learning habits?

9&10 Review 5

Vocabulary

1 Circle the correct option to complete each sentence.

1 It's easy to *sail / take* a bus in this city.

2 He *drives / rides* a bike to school every day.

3 Do you know how to *drive / fly* a car?

4 I want to learn how to *ride / sail* a boat.

5 Can I *take / fly* a train to Lisbon?

2 Complete the sentences with these words.

rain	snow	sun	wind

1 Look at all the _____! Let's go skiing.

2 Take an umbrella. Don't get wet in the _____.

3 The _____ is out. It's really hot now.

4 The _____ is strong. Let's go sailing!

3 Circle the correct body part.

1 You wear a shoe on this.   *head / foot*

2 You see with this.   *head / eye*

3 You listen with this.   *ear / mouth*

4 You hold things with this.   *eye / hand*

5 You wear a hat on this.   *foot / head*

4 Circle the correct option to complete each sentence.

1 Luke is *practicing / preparing* the piano right now.

2 Erica is *learning / exercising* Spanish online.

3 Yvonne is *practicing / exercising* more to be healthy.

4 Khalid is *learning / preparing* for a big tennis match tomorrow.

Grammar

1 Circle the correct options to complete the conversation.

Teotihuacan, Mexico

A: Jorge, can you help ¹*me / I* ? What are some fun things to do in Mexico City?

B: Well, there ²*is / are* the pyramids of Teotihuacan. They aren't in the city, but they are near ³*it / them*.

A: ⁴*Is / Are* there a bus to the pyramids?

B: Yes, but there ⁵*is / are* lots of tours you can take, too. You can find ⁶*us / them* online.

A: What about food? ⁷*Is / Are* there any good restaurants?

B: There are ⁸*any / many* amazing restaurants! There's ⁹*one / some* called "Pujol."

2 Complete the email with the simple present or present continuous form of the verbs in parentheses.

Hi Jack,

How are you? I'm finally in Tbilisi, Georgia, and I ¹_____ (stay) in a nice hotel. I ²_____ (love) all the beautiful streets and buildings. I often ³_____ (walk) around the city and ⁴_____ (take) photos. Right now, I ⁵_____ (look) for great places to eat in the city. Let's ⁶_____ (visit) some of them together!

Lots of love,
Lucy

Reading

1 Read the blog post. Who is it for? Circle the correct answer.

a dancers   b fitness trainers c health workers

2 Read the blog post again. Complete the sentences with words from it.

1 The writer dances two or three times a _____.

2 The dance group's _____ help tell its story.

3 The writer says dancing is like a _____.

4 Breathing exercises help the writer _____.

My life as a dancer

I travel to one or two dance competitions every month, and right now I'm getting ready for a big one! There are many ways to prepare for a competition, but let me tell you what I'm doing.

Practice!
I usually dance two or three times a week, but right now I'm practicing every day. And it's not just me. My dance group really wants to win, so we're all working really hard.

Wear the right clothes
In dance, what you wear is really important. We use our clothes to help tell our story. So we're also working very hard on what to wear.

Be healthy
Dancing is like a sport. You need to be fit. Right now, I'm exercising a lot and I'm avoiding unhealthy foods, too.

Travel
My dance group has twenty members and our competition is in a different city. I'm team leader, so it's my job to get everyone there. I'm looking for bus and train tickets for us and all our equipment.

Relax
It's easy to worry before a competition. Many things can go wrong, but it's very important to relax. I like breathing exercises for this.

Dance competitions are really difficult, but they're great fun, too. They also teach you a lot. If you want to become a better dancer, try joining a dance competition!

Listening

1 🎧 R5.1 Listen to part of a bus tour of Athens. Circle the places that are mentioned.

Athens

| National Gardens | National Library |
| Panathenaic Stadium | Syntagma Square |

2 🎧 R5.1 Listen again. Circle the correct option to complete each sentence.

1 There are benches for *picnics* / *pictures* at the National Gardens of Athens.

2 There is a small *building* / *zoo* here where you can visit the animals.

3 The first Olympic Games were held in *1896* / *1996* at the Panathenaic Stadium.

4 The Panathenaic Stadium has *55,000* / *50,000* seats.

Pronunciation

1 🎧 R5.2 Listen and circle the word you hear.

1 four   fourth   3 eighteen eighteenth

2 thirteen thirteenth   4 twenty   twentieth

2 🎧 R5.3 Listen to the intonation. Then complete the directions.

1 Go to the café, turn _____, then turn _____.

2 Walk that way, turn _____, and go _____.

3 Go straight, turn left at the _____, and turn left again at the _____.

4 Turn left, turn right at the _____, and go straight on _____ Street.

11 People from the past

Vocabulary

Life events

1 Complete the text with these words.

died   lived   was born

Writer Jane Austen [1]_____ a short, but interesting life. She [2]_____ in Hampshire, U.K., on December 16, 1775 and she [3]_____ on July 18, 1817. She was only 41 years old. Some of her books, like *Emma* and *Pride and Prejudice*, are also movies.

2 Circle the correct options to complete the text.

Austen was a writer [1]*ago / for / from* many years. She wrote her most famous books [2]*ago / for / from* 1811 to 1815. She was born over 200 years [3]*ago / for / from*, but her books are still popular today.

Reading

1 Skim the movie review on page 75. What does the reviewer think about the movie? Circle the correct answer.

a The reviewer loves it.

b The reviewer thinks it's OK.

c The reviewer hates it.

2 Read the review. Circle the event (a or b) that happens first.

1 a Selena joined her family band.

   b Selena was born.

2 a Selena died.

   b Selena married Chris Perez.

3 Complete the sentences.

1 Tejano is a mix of _____ and American music.

2 Selena was born in _____ in 1971.

3 Selena recorded her first _____ in 1989.

4 Chris Perez was a _____ in the band.

5 Jennifer Lopez doesn't _____ in the movie.

Look at the Learning to Learn box. Then do the task.

LEARNING TO LEARN: READING

Facts and opinions

A fact is true for everyone. An opinion is something you think or believe—it is not a fact. Some texts have both. When you read, try to see which statements are facts and which are opinions.

Look at these sentences from the movie review. Circle F (fact) or O (opinion).

1 "I don't usually review old movies."   (F)   O

2 "Selena made her first album in 1989."   F   O

3 "Selena died on March 31, 1995."   F   O

4 "I think she was excellent as Selena."   F   O

5 "I feel that Jennifer Lopez's acting is very good."   F   O

6 "The singing voice you hear is Selena's."   F   O

Movie review: *Selena*

★★★★★

Today, I'm doing something different. I don't usually review old movies, but everyone says this movie was amazing. So this week's movie is *Selena*. The 1997 film tells the story of Selena Quintanilla, a famous Tejano singer. (Tejano is a mix of American and Mexican music.)

Selena was born in Texas on April 16, 1971. She was in a band with her family from the 1980s to the early 1990s. The movie shows the band on the road and in concerts in Texas and Mexico. The band was very popular, but Selena was the star. She made her first album in 1989.

Selena was in love with Chris Perez, the band's guitarist. By 1992, they were husband and wife. Selena's father was not happy about this. The ending of the movie was very sad. Selena died on March 31, 1995. She was only 23 years old.

Selena Quintanilla singing on stage

Jennifer Lopez acting in the movie *Selena*

The movie stars Jennifer Lopez as Selena. I think she was excellent. It was one of her first movie roles. I feel that Jennifer Lopez's acting is very good. You believe she *is* Selena. Lopez is also a great singer, but she doesn't sing in the movie. The singing voice you hear is Selena's.

I hope people watch this movie. It's a beautiful story of an amazing star who died too young. I give the film 5 stars.

Grammar

Simple past *be*

1 Circle the correct option to complete each sentence.

1 He *was / were* famous as a child.

2 Her grandparents *was / were* from Russia.

3 You *wasn't / weren't* in class yesterday.

4 My brother *wasn't / weren't* angry with me.

5 She *was / were* born in 2001.

6 They *wasn't / weren't* friends in school.

2 Put the words in order to make sentences.

1 were / last year / in / the same class / we

_____

2 at the movie theater / last night / I / was

_____

3 flute / wasn't / bag / her / in / Grace's

_____

4 weren't / yesterday / my parents / at home

_____

3 Complete the text with the simple past of *be*.

My grandmother [1]_____*was*_____ (be) an artist. She [2]_____ (be) an album-cover designer from 1960 to 1968. Her designs [3]_____ (be / not) like other album covers from that time. They [4]_____ (be) always black and white and there usually [5]_____ (be / not) any people on them. Her covers [6]_____ (be / not) very famous, but I really love her interesting designs.

Pronunciation

Understanding *was* and *were*

1 🔊 **11.1** Listen and circle the word you hear.

1 was   were   3 was   were

2 was   were   4 was   were

Ali Farka Touré singing

Vocabulary

Past time expressions

1 Circle the correct option to complete each sentence.

1 I didn't sleep much last *night / year*. I'm very tired today.

2 Martha Graham was a famous dancer from the 20th *year / century*.

3 We were at an amazing art show *last / yesterday* week.

4 Artist Katsushika Hokusai died in the *year / century* 1849.

5 Diego Rivera was a famous painter from *last night / the last century*.

2 Read the sentences. Are they true (T) or false (F)?

1 Last year was the year before this year.   T   F

2 Last week was the week before this week.   T   F

3 An event from last night was two days ago.   T   F

4 The year 1992 was in the 19th century.   T   F

5 The year 1850 was in the last century.   T   F

6 The year 2010 is in this century.   T   F

Listening

1 🎧 11.2 Listen to a conversation about the musician Ali Farka Touré. Check (✓) the things the people talk about.

a ☐ where he was born

b ☐ his family

c ☐ his favorite singer

d ☐ his music

e ☐ his first album

2 🎧 11.2 Listen again. Are the sentences true (T) or false (F)?

1 Ali Farka Touré was born in France.   T   F

2 He played many musical instruments.   T   F

3 He was a good guitar player.   T   F

4 He was a farmer.   T   F

5 He died in 2016.   T   F

6 His album *Talking Timbuktu* sold 150,000 copies in the U.S.   T   F

Grammar

Questions with *was / were*

1 Complete the questions with *was* or *were*.

1 _____ the Olympics in Turin in 2006?

2 _____ Vancouver the Olympic city in 2014?

3 _____ the Olympics in Sochi in 2018?

4 When _____ Pyeongchang the host city?

5 Where _____ the Olympics in 2010?

6 What _____ the Olympic country in 2014?

7 _____ there any Olympic Games in 2007?

2 Look at the timeline. Match the questions (1–7) in Exercise 1 with the answers (a–g) below.

a No, it wasn't.   ___2___

b Russia.   _____

c In 2018.   _____

d Yes, they were.   _____

e In Vancouver.   _____

f No, they weren't.   _____

g No, there weren't.   _____

Winter Olympic Cities

Turin, Italy	Vancouver, Canada	Sochi, Russia	Pyeongchang, South Korea
2006	2010	2014	2018

3 Circle the correct options to complete the conversation.

A: Do you know much about Ibn Battuta? He's really interesting. I'm doing a report on him.

B: I'm not sure. ¹*Was / Were* he an explorer?

A: Yes, but he was also a writer.

B: Where ²*was / were* he from?

A: Morocco. His travels were really amazing—from Morocco to Arabia, Africa, and all over Asia.

B: Wow! ³*Was / Were* that just one trip?

A: No, he took three different journeys.

B: ⁴*Was / Were* the trips exciting?

A: Of course!

Ibn Battuta in Egypt

Pronunciation

Responding to good and bad news

1 🔊 11.3 Listen to people responding to news. Is the news good or bad? Circle the correct answers.

1 good news	bad news
2 good news	bad news
3 good news	bad news
4 good news	bad news

2 🔊 11.3 Listen again and repeat.

Look at the Learning to Learn box. Then do the task.

LEARNING TO LEARN: PRONUNCIATION

Checking pronunciation
Sometimes, it's useful to check a word's pronunciation. But be careful! Some words can have different pronunciations. Some words …

1 have one meaning, with two possible pronunciations.
2 have more than one meaning, with different pronunciations.
3 sound different in different parts of the world (e.g., the U.S. and the U.K.).

Look up these words in a dictionary. Write the correct numbers from the Learning to Learn box above (1–3) next them.

a record _____   b either _____   c often _____

Astronaut Ellen Ochoa in the SpaceHab module

Writing

1 Match the information from a profile of Ellen Ochoa (a–h) with the sections (1–3). More than one answer may be possible.

1 The introduction   _____

2 Important life events   _____

3 Why she's special   _____

a first Hispanic woman to go to space

b born in Los Angeles in 1958

c was an astronaut

d was director at Johnson Space Center

e always interested in space

f was in space for nine days

g first trip to space was in 1993

h is now a very popular speaker

2 You are going to write a profile about Ellen Ochoa. Make notes using the three sections in Exercise 1 to help you.

3 Use your notes in Exercise 2 to write a profile of Ellen Ochoa.

4 Check your profile. Use the checklist.

☐ Are the spelling and punctuation correct?

☐ Are the grammar and vocabulary correct?

☐ Does your profile include all the information from your notes in Exercise 2?

Look at the Learning to Learn box. Complete your learning journal.

LEARNING TO LEARN: YOUR LEARNING JOURNAL

You're almost at the end of the Student's Book. Now is a good time to think about your learning and your progress. Look back at your other journal entries. Then write or record a new entry in your journal. Use these questions to help you.

1 **What are some areas you feel good about? Think about reading, writing, speaking, listening, grammar, and vocabulary.**
   I feel good about … because …

2 **What areas were difficult for you? Are they easier for you now?**
   … was difficult before, but it's easier now.

3 **What do you want to improve? What do you need to review?**
   I want to improve …
   I need to review …

12 My story

Vocabulary

Life stages

1 Circle the correct options to make phrases.

1 *go to / live in* college

2 *get / buy* a job

3 *have / get* married

4 *start / go* a business

5 *get / finish* college

6 *buy / go* a house

7 *start / have* children

8 *get / live in* another country

2 Complete the sentences with the phrases from Exercise 1.

1 Let's _____. We can open a small café or a restaurant.

2 Your daughters are beautiful. My husband and I plan to _____ soon.

3 I'd like to _____ this summer and save some money.

4 I want to _____ some day. I think Spain is nice, or maybe Italy.

5 It's not easy to _____ in this neighborhood. They're very expensive.

6 Delia wants to _____, but she didn't do well in school.

7 Jackie hopes to _____ soon. She needs to take three more classes.

8 Jen and Marc want to _____ on the beach. They don't want to invite many people.

Reading

1 Skim the article on page 81. What is it about? Circle the correct answer.

a a blogger who lived in the Seychelles for ten years

b the first Black woman to visit every country in the world

c job experience in the United Nations

2 Read the article. Match the sentence beginnings (1–4) with the endings (a–d).

1 Jessica was born in _____   a Indonesia.

2 She lived for a year in _____   b the Seychelles.

3 In 2017, she visited _____   c Japan.

4 In 2019, she went to _____   d the U.S.

3 Read the sentences. Are they true (T) or false (F)?

1 Jessica was born in 1984.   T   F

2 She was a teacher in Indonesia.   T   F

3 In 2019, the last country Jessica visited   T   F
  was Singapore.

4 For Jessica, an important part of   T   F
  traveling is meeting people.

4 How many voices does the article have?

a One   b Two   c Three

Pronunciation

Saying syllables with two vowel sounds

1 🔊 12.1 Listen. Do the two words have the same vowel sound? Circle yes (Y) or no (N).

1 boy how Y N   3 now out Y N

2 here dear Y N   4 toy wow Y N

2 🔊 12.1 Listen again and repeat.

JESSICA NABONGO
World traveler

Jessica Nabongo is a blogger and photographer. And she loves visiting new places.

Jessica was born in 1984 in the United States. She lived and studied there and, when she finished college, she got a job in sales. But she was soon bored. She decided she wanted to live in another country, and so she moved to Japan to teach English. After a year in Japan, she moved to London.

Jessica then got a job in the United Nations. She learned a lot, but she wanted more: she wanted to travel again. In 2017, she went to Bali, Indonesia on vacation. She decided there that she wanted to visit every country in the world. She quit her job and traveled for the next two years. In 2019, she visited her last country—the Seychelles. She became the first Black woman to visit every country in the world.

Jessica is proud of this, but for her, traveling is not just about how many countries she visits. It's about the people she meets and what she learns.

Grammar

Simple past (regular verbs)

1 Write the simple past forms of the verbs.

	Positive	**Negative**
1 study	_studied_	_didn't study_
2 work	_____	_____
3 help	_____	_____
4 live	_____	_____
5 talk	_____	_____
6 stop	_____	_____

2 Complete the sentences. Use the simple past form of the verbs in parentheses.

1 We ___watched___ (watch) two movies last night.

2 She _____ (not / play) soccer at school.

3 It _____ (rain) all day yesterday.

4 They _____ (not / walk) to the concert.

5 He _____ (live) in Spain in 2019.

6 I _____ (not / like) last night's dinner at all.

3 Did you do these things last weekend? Write complete sentences that are true for you.

1 study

   I didn't study last weekend.

2 play golf

   _____

3 shop online

   _____

4 watch TV

   _____

5 talk to friends

   _____

Grammar

Simple past (irregular verbs)

1 Match these irregular verbs with the base forms (1–6).

felt   ran   sent   thought   took   woke

1 take _____   4 send _____

2 wake _____   5 think _____

3 run _____   6 feel _____

2 Circle the correct option to complete each sentence.

1 I *fall* / *fell* asleep on the couch last night.

2 She *get* / *got* up at 6:00 a.m.

3 We *became* / *become* very good friends.

4 He didn't *give* / *gave* me his email address.

5 I didn't *saw* / *see* her at the beach last weekend.

3 Look at the sentences in Exercise 2 again. Make sentences 1–3 negative, and sentences 4–5 positive.

1 *I didn't fall asleep on the couch last night.*

2 _____

3 _____

4 _____

5 _____

Listening

1 🔊 12.2 Listen to a woman telling a funny story. Are the sentences true (T) or false (F)?

1 This is a true story.	T F
2 The woman didn't eat breakfast.	T F
3 The woman took a bus to university.	T F
4 The teacher was angry at the woman.	T F
5 The woman texted her teacher.	T F

2 🔊 **12.2** Listen again. What makes the story funny? Circle the correct answer.

a She woke up an hour late.

b She thought it was a different day.

c She went to the wrong university.

Look at the Learning to Learn box. Then do the task.

Listen to one or more audio tracks from this book. Think about these questions.

- Is this accent similar to your accent?

- Is it easy for you to understand? Why or why not?

- Where can you get more practice with this type of accent?

Grammar

Simple past questions

1 Put the words in order to make questions.

1 walk / did / to school / he

Did he walk to school ?

2 you / did / your hair / change

_____?

3 say / that / why / did / you

_____?

4 in Brazil / did / you and Ben / live / when

_____?

5 did / play / what sports / she / at school

_____?

2 Correct the mistake in each question.

1 Did you **went** to the market?

Did you go to the market?

2 When Chi **did** live in Japan?

_____

3 **Do** you see your parents last weekend?

_____

4 What time did they **got** home?

_____

3 Complete the conversation with the simple past form of the verbs in parentheses.

A: Where ¹ *did you live* (you / live) as a child?

B: I ² _____ (born) in Panama, and I ³ _____ (live) there for five years. Then we ⁴ _____ (move) to Canada.

A: Canada? Interesting. How ⁵ _____ (you / like) it there?

B: Well, I ⁶ _____ (not / like) it at first, but I love it now.

A: ⁷ _____ (be) you a good student?

B: Yes, I was. I ⁸ _____ (study) all the time.

Pronunciation

Stressing words in questions

1 🔊 **12.3** Listen and underline the stressed words.

1 Did it rain?

2 Did he cook this?

3 Where did they walk?

4 Why did she say that?

5 Did you enjoy it?

2 🔊 **12.3** Listen again and repeat.

Vocabulary

Feelings

1 Match the pictures (1–8) with the adjectives (a–h).

1 _____ a angry

2 _____ b surprised

3 _____ c happy

4 _____ d tired

5 _____ e sad

6 _____ f excited

7 _____ g bored

8 _____ h afraid

2 Circle the correct option to complete each sentence.

1 I got an A in math! I'm really *sad / surprised / bored*. I never get an A!

2 Jeff dropped my cellphone and it broke. I'm so *angry / excited / tired*.

3 I woke up late and ran to work. I'm so *angry / tired / bored* now.

4 I'm *afraid / happy / bored*. There is nothing fun to do around here.

5 Leona gave me a new hat for my birthday! I'm really *angry / happy / tired*.

6 Chai is *bored / surprised / afraid* of the lions in the zoo.

7 I can't play soccer now because it's raining outside. I'm *excited / happy / sad*.

Writing

1 Read the sentences about someone's grandfather. Each set (1–3) contains one main idea and two interesting points. Circle M (main idea) or I (interesting point) for each sentence.

1 a He lived a very interesting and exciting life. Ⓜ I

  b He lived in many different countries. M I

  c He met many famous people. M I

2 a There weren't many buildings or cars. M I

  b Life was very different in the 1950s. M I

  c Nobody had TVs in their homes. M I

3 a He teaches his grandchildren many things. M I

  b He always tells us great stories. M I

  c Our lives changed when he moved in with us. M I

2 Find out about the life of a family member or someone you know. Complete the table with main ideas and add one or two interesting points for each.

	Main idea	Interesting points
As a child		
As a teenager		
As an adult		

3 Write the life story of the person from Exercise 2. Use your notes in Exercise 2 to help you. Write 50–75 words. Use the tips below to help you.

- Write one or two interesting points for each main idea.
- Use adjectives to say how things looked or felt.

Look at the Learning to Learn box. Then do the task.

LEARNING TO LEARN: WRITING

Describing people, places, or things

When you describe a person, place, or thing, think about how you can help the reader see it in their mind. For example, imagine you're writing about a room. Is the room big or small? Is it dark or full of light? What colors are there? Who or what is in the room? Give interesting details to help the reader imagine what you're describing.

Look at your writing in Exercise 3. How can you help the reader see the things you're describing? What details do you want to add?

4 Check the life story. Use the checklist.

☐ Are the spelling and punctuation correct?

☐ Are the grammar and vocabulary correct?

☐ Does your story include all the information from the notes in Exercise 2?

Look at the Learning to Learn box. Then do the task.

LEARNING TO LEARN: PREPARING FOR TESTS

Students often need to take tests. Tests can show what you know well and where you can improve. Try these tips when preparing for a test.

Start early

- Start studying early.
- Review your textbook. Where do you need to improve?
- Try a few practice tests. Ask your teacher or find them online.

Before the test

- Get a good night's sleep before the test.
- Eat. You don't want to feel hungry during your test.

During the test

- Look through the test quickly. Which questions need more time?
- Read the instructions carefully.
- Check your answers.

After the test

- Check where you did well and where you didn't.
- Practice the language points you need to improve on.

Make notes on these questions.

1 Which tips for tests do you already follow?

_____

2 Which tips don't you follow? Do you think they're useful?

_____

3 What other tips can you add to the list?

_____

11&12 Review 6

Vocabulary

1 Circle the correct options to complete the text.

Ella Fitzgerald was a famous jazz singer from the early 20th [1]*year / century*. She [2]*was born / lived* in the U.S. in 1917, over a hundred years [3]*ago / for*. She had an amazing talent for music. In 1934, she performed at Harlem's famous Apollo Theater. It was her first big show. Fitzgerald sang on stage [4]*for / from* nearly 60 years. She [5]*died / dead in* 1996.

2 Complete the sentences with these words.

buy	finish	get	get	go	have	live	start

1 Katie wants to _____ to college in France and then _____ a business.

2 After Kenji and Erica _____ married, they hope to _____ children.

3 Lacey wants to _____ a job and _____ in another country for a few years.

4 Don't _____ a house now. They're expensive. Please _____ college first.

3 Complete the sentences with these words.

sad	excited	tired
bored	surprised	happy

1 Emma and Joanne have nothing to do. They're _____.

2 Bernadette's cat died last night. She's very _____.

3 Omar didn't know his hotel had free breakfasts. He was _____.

4 Today is my first day at my dream job. I'm very _____!

5 Dana worked from 10 p.m to 7 a.m. Now she's _____.

6 George loves his new job at the college. He's very _____.

Grammar

1 Circle the correct option to complete each sentence.

1 We *was / were* late for our dance lesson.

2 Edvard Munch *was / were* a Norwegian painter.

3 *Was / Were* you happy with the book's ending?

4 How *was / were* your trip to Switzerland?

5 Her paintings *wasn't / weren't* very good.

6 Why *wasn't / weren't* Mandy in class yesterday?

2 Complete the conversation with the simple past form of the verbs in parentheses.

A: [1]_____ (you / go) to the outdoor concert yesterday?

B: Yes, I did. I [2]_____ (love) it. The musicians [3]_____ (play) beautifully.

A: [4]_____ (Becca / join) you?

B: No. She [5]_____ (not / have) the day off, so I [6]_____ (ask) Sun-hee.

A: What [7]_____ (you / do) after the concert?

B: We [8]_____ (take) a walk around the park and then [9]_____ (stop) at a café.

A: [10]_____ (you / eat) there?

B: No, we just [11]_____ (have) coffee.

Reading

1 Read the article. Who did these things?
Circle H (Hercules) or R (Robin Hood).

1 lived in a forest   H   R

2 lived in Greece   H   R

3 fought several animals   H   R

4 helped poor people   H   R

2 Correct the mistake in each sentence.

1 Hercules was strong and **funny**.   _____

2 Robin Hood gave **food** to people.   _____

Always the Hero

*They are in many books and movies, but
did these early heroes really live, or are the
stories of their lives just that—stories?*

Hercules

Hercules was a great
hero from Greece. He
was famous for being
very strong. As a baby, he
found two large snakes
in his bed. He picked
them up and threw
them out. Hercules was
also clever. He once needed to clean the
stables of 3,000 cows in one day. He moved
two rivers so they quickly washed over the
area. Hercules had many other adventures,
including fighting a lion.

Robin Hood

Robin Hood lived in a
forest near Nottingham,
U.K. He was a kind man
and had an easy life. He
and his group of friends
didn't like following rules.
They preferred playing
games and having fun.
Robin Hood was a hero to poor people, but
not to rich people. He took money from the
rich and gave it to the poor. Many people in
Nottingham tried to catch Robin Hood, but
they never did.

Listening

1 🎧 R6.1 Listen to the conversation. Number
the questions in the order you hear them.

a _____ What did he do?

b _____ How many copies did he make?

c _____ Did you say anything?

d _____ Why are you smiling?

2 🎧 R6.1 Listen again and complete the summary.
Ken is part of Natasha's team. She asked him to
make ¹_____ copies for her, but he only
²_____ 50. He said he was sorry and
³_____ the ⁴_____ copies
in the recycling bin. Then he went and made
100 new ones!

Pronunciation

1 🎧 R6.2 Listen and mark the bold words
S (strong form) or W (weak form).

A: **Were** you at the meeting?   S   W

B: Yes, we **were**.   S   W

A: **Was** it interesting?   S   W

B: It **was**.   S   W

2 🎧 R6.3 Listen and circle the stressed words.

1 a Did **she like** it?   b **Did** she **like** it?

2 a **What** did you **say**?   b What **did you** say?

3 a **Did** they **see** me?   b **Did** they see **me**?

4 a Where did **he go**?   b **Where** did he **go**?

Audioscripts

UNIT 1

1.1

1 Toronto
2 Japan
3 Lima
4 Argentina
5 Vietnam
6 Washington

1.2

Conversation 1
A: Excuse me, Lenora. What's your phone number?
B: It's 662-0904-1331.
A: Is that 662-0904-1331?
B: Yes, that's right.

Conversation 2
A: Good morning. I'm Marcy Taylor. My bank account number is 445-729-13-99.
B: I'm sorry. Can I have that again please?
A: 445-729-13-99.
B: Ah, yes. Marcy Taylor. And how can I help you?

Conversation 3
A: Hello, I'm Greg Iverson. How are you?
B: I'm fine, thanks. What's your student number?
A: It's 839-155-702.
B: 839-155-720?
A: No, sorry. It's 702, not 720.

1.3

1 I'm Dana. I'm from Canada.
2 I'm from Portugal. I'm not from Spain.
3 Are you French? I'm French, too.

UNIT 2

2.1

1 I am
2 You are
3 He's
4 She is
5 It's
6 We're
7 They are

2.2

A: Hello, Idris!
B: Hi, Celia. How are you?
A: I'm great, thanks. And you?
B: Not bad. Wow. Is that your apartment? It's very nice!
A: Yes, it is. Thanks!
B: Where are you? Is that your bedroom?
A: No, it's not. I'm in the living room.
B: I see! Is your apartment big?
A: No, it isn't—not for two people. I share the apartment with Antonia. There's a living room, two bedrooms, a small kitchen, and a tiny bathroom.
B: Oh. Who's Antonia?
A: She's an old friend. She's from Veracruz.
B: Veracruz? Where's Veracruz?
A: It's in Mexico. It's a big city.

2.3

1 Is it over there?
2 It's next to the school.
3 Is it on Main Street?
4 It's near the school.
5 It's in the mall.
6 It's under the table?

1&2 REVIEW 1

R1.1

My name is Wendy. I live in an apartment, next to a nice park. It's near the bus station, too. My apartment has three rooms: a kitchen, a bathroom, and a living room. It doesn't have a dining room or a bedroom—my bed is in the living room. My apartment is small, but that's OK. It's cheap and it's easy to clean. I love it!

R1.2

1 ci-ty
2 sho-wer
3 sta-tion
4 mu-se-um
5 su-per-mar-ket
6 af-ter-noon

1 it is
2 who's
3 isn't
4 we're

UNIT 3

3.1

1 that
2 these
3 they
4 this
5 the
6 those

3.2

A: Hi, Dani.
B: Oh, hi, Ian. How are you?
A: I'm great. What's that?
B: It's a photo of my new car. I love it!
A: That's an interesting color.
B: Yeah, it's pink!
A: Is pink your favorite color?
B: No, it's not. I like pink, but red is my favorite color.
A: Ahh. Who's that with you? In the green and blue T-shirt?
B: Oh, that's my friend Jasmine.
A: I love her T-shirt. The colors are nice.
B: All her T-shirts are amazing. She designs T-shirts. Here … This is her website …
A: Wow. These are cool. I like that one … the green and orange T-shirt. And that one, too … the orange and black one … Is orange her favorite color?
B: Yes, it is.

3.3

1 Your teacher is here.
2 You're late for school.
3 Their house is white.
4 They're from India.

UNIT 4

4.1

1 bus stop
2 number
3 money
4 hundred
5 under
6 running

4.2

A: So tell me, Dad … What do you usually do on the weekend?
B: Well, I usually work on Saturdays. I get up at 8, and I drive to the office. I come home at 1:00. I always have lunch with your mother. Then I usually exercise.
A: And what do you do in the evening?
B: I usually read, but sometimes your mother and I watch a movie.
A: And what about Sunday?
B: On Sundays? I get up at about 11 o'clock—I never get up early on Sundays. Then I meet my friends. We always have lunch together.
A: That sounds fun. What do you do on Sunday night?
B: I usually have a small dinner with you and your mom, and then I rest.
A: That's great, Dad. Thanks for the interview!
B: You're welcome!

4.3

1 huge
2 excuse
3 music
4 Sunday
5 umbrella
6 university

3&4 REVIEW 2

R2.1

Interviewer: Charlene, thanks for doing this interview.
Charlene: You're very welcome, Matt. I'm happy to be here.
Interviewer: Please tell us … What's your hobby?
Charlene: Well, I have a metal detector. I use it to find metal things in the ground. I usually find keys, drink cans—things like that. But sometimes I find some really interesting things, like this watch.

Audioscripts

Interviewer: Wow. That's a nice watch! Where do you go to look for things?
Charlene: I usually go to the beach. Sometimes, I drive to different places far from the city.
Interviewer: I see. When do you go out?
Charlene: On weekends. I usually go out on Sunday mornings.
Interviewer: Why do you like this hobby?
Charlene: I think it's fun. And sometimes, I help people. I find phones, bags, or wallets, and I return them.
Interviewer: That's nice. Is it an expensive hobby?
Charlene: Well, good metal detectors are expensive, but I use my father's.

R2.2

1 You're in this class.
2 Their bags are in the bedroom.

R2.3

1 run
2 you
3 fun
4 future
5 lunch
6 music

UNIT 5

5.1

1 playing
2 climbing
3 listening
4 cycling
5 chatting
6 drawing

5.2

Cory: Hi, Mia. Would you like to do something fun this weekend?
Mia: This weekend? Sure. What do you want to do?
Cory: I don't know. Do you like playing video games?
Mia: I do, but it's summer. Let's do something outside.
Cory: OK. Do you want to play basketball?
Mia: No. I don't like playing basketball.
Cory: How about cycling?
Mia: Yes, I love cycling. And I have a new bicycle.

Cory: Great. Is Saturday afternoon OK?
Mia: Sorry, but I'm busy. How about Sunday afternoon?
Cory: OK. When is a good time for you?
Mia: Is 3 p.m. OK?
Cory: No. I work from 11 to 3. How about 4 p.m.?
Mia: Sunday at 4 is great. Let's meet at school.
Cory: How about the park? It's near my house.
Mia: Perfect! See you then!

5.3

1 Who would you like to see?
2 What would you like to do?
3 What would you like to eat?
4 Where would you like to go?

UNIT 6

6.1

1 a slice of bread
2 a cup of tea
3 a lot of rice
4 a teaspoon of salt
5 a bar of chocolate

6.2

People put about 30% of the food they buy in the trash. They just throw it away! What about you? Do you waste food? Answer these questions to find out.

1: Do you make shopping lists?
People without shopping lists often buy more groceries. They buy too much food and they don't eat all of it. Some of the food goes bad.

2: How often do you go to the supermarket?
Many people shop for groceries once or twice a month. They buy a lot of food. And they keep it longer, so more of it goes bad. Go to the supermarket once or twice a week, and don't buy a lot when you're there.

3: Do you bring home the food you don't finish at restaurants?
When people at restaurants don't finish their food, the restaurants just throw it away. Ask the waiter to pack up the food you don't finish, and take it home with you.
Remember these tips and you can waste less food!

🎧 6.3
1 hello
2 help
3 have
4 how much
5 how many

5&6 REVIEW 3

🎧 R3.1

Natasha: Hello, everyone! This is Natasha at Radio KZ29. Tomorrow is the start of summer. We want to know: What do you like doing in the summer? Let's take a caller.

Zac: Hi, Natasha. This is Zac. I like hiking with my family. I love being outdoors!

Natasha: What about camping? Do you like sleeping in a tent?

Zac: Hmm. I love camping, but not in the summer. It's hot. I usually camp in the spring.

Natasha: That's interesting. Thank you, Zac. Let's take another caller.

Julia: Hello? Is that you, Natasha?

Natasha: Yes, it is. And what's your name?

Julia: My name's Julia and I love, love, love going to the beach and swimming.

Natasha: Where do you live, Julia? We don't have any nice beaches here.

Julia: I live here in Atlanta. And you're right—we don't have any nice beaches. But I love driving down to Jacksonville. It's 550 kilometers away, but they have an amazing beach. Come with us sometime!

Natasha: Thanks, Julia. But I'm an indoor person. I love playing video games and eating pizza. I don't like running around in the sun!

🎧 R3.2

1 What would you like to see?
2 Where would you like to go?
3 When would you like to eat?
4 Who would you like to visit?

🎧 R3.3

1 riding
2 eating
3 doing
4 camping

UNIT 7

🎧 7.1

1 hat   hate
2 teen   ten
3 bit   bite
4 note   not
5 cute   cut

🎧 7.2

Hello. I'm Sara Sanchez, and welcome to this week's podcast. Today, I want to talk about friends. Everyone needs friends. But what makes a good friend?

A friend can be tall or short. They can look just like you, or they can look very different. Appearance is not important. But personality is important.

Here are five things you want in a good friend. One: a good friend is nice. They're kind to you, and to others, too. Two: a good friend listens. They're interested in your life, and all the things that happen to you. Three: a good friend makes you laugh. Funny people make everything fun—even the things you don't enjoy. Four: a good friend is always there for you. You can call, text, or meet them any time. That's the difference between a friend, and a good friend. Five: a good friend doesn't lie—they say what's true. Eighty percent of people say this is very important … and I agree.

🎧 7.3

1 Antonio often makes me laugh. He's funny.
2 Jessica does very well at school. She's clever.
3 Antonio is kind and easy to talk to. He's nice.
4 Jessica has a lot of ideas. She's never boring. She's interesting.
5 Sometimes, Antonio doesn't talk much. He's quiet.

Audioscripts

🎧 7.4

1 green
2 practice
3 agree
4 going
5 hungry
6 cry

🎧 7.5

1 group
2 grade
3 agree
4 grocery
5 kilogram
6 grandson

UNIT 8

🎧 8.1

1 He can cook.
2 They can't swim.
3 She can ride a bike.
4 We can't run a marathon.
5 I can't play the piano.
6 He can stand on his head.

🎧 8.2

Simone: Hello, everyone, and welcome. I'm your guide Simone, and I'm here to tell you all about the animals at our Australian wildlife park.
Let's start with kangaroos. These animals are from Australia, and they're amazing. They can run 60 kilometers an hour, and they can jump nine meters! One interesting fact—kangaroos can't walk backwards.

Guest: Really? That's interesting. Can kangaroos swim?

Simone: Great question. Yes, they can. They're great swimmers. They use their strong tails to swim. Next, we have koalas. Some people call them koala bears, but they're not bears. They're a different type of animal. Koalas can sleep up to 22 hours a day, high up in the trees. That's why we don't see them often. They're really cute, but be careful—sometimes they're dangerous. Another animal here at our park is the camel …

Guest: Camels? Are camels from Australia?

Simone: No, they aren't, but we have many camels in Australia now. Camels are amazing. They're fast. They can run 40 kilometers an hour. And they don't drink often. But when they do, they can drink about 200 liters of water in three minutes!

🎧 8.3

1 huge
2 doing
3 game
4 amazing
5 yoga
6 orange

7&8 REVIEW 4

🎧 R4.1

Are you interested in movies, and do you want to learn how to make one? Then join us at Star Studios for our amazing three-month summer job program.

What are you good at? Are you a writer? Can you make great music? Or can you draw and paint? We have all kinds of jobs for people with different interests and abilities.

Work on real movie sets, and learn from real writers, directors, and actors. Find out what happens behind the cameras, and see your work end up on the movie screen. There's no other summer job like it!

So what are you waiting for? Visit our website and complete our online form today. You'll get a room to live in, three meals a day, and money for transportation and everyday needs.

Don't wait. Visit the Star Studio website today. (If you're under 18, please get permission from a parent.)

🎧 R4.2

1 man	hat
2 bed	when
3 him	wife
4 not	goes
5 but	run

1 Hal can't play the piano well.
2 Kaley can count to ten in five languages.
3 Dmitri can fix your computer.
4 Shweta can't swim.
5 David can't sing, but he can dance.

UNIT 9

9.1

Advertisement 1
Do you love seeing wildlife? Then come to Chitwan National Park in Nepal. Walk around the park or travel by boat. Look for elephants, snakes, birds, and even tigers. Come between October and March—the weather is warm and sunny then. Try not to visit in the summer. That's the rainy season, so it's not easy to get around. Call us for more information.

Advertisement 2
Why not take a tour with us to Samaria National Park, in Greece? This park on the island of Crete is a great place to spend a day. People go to Samaria to hike. Start early for the 16-kilometer walk through the rocky passage. Enjoy the views, and then swim in the ocean. Hike between May and October. And don't worry: The hike is all downhill! Email us to find out more.

Advertisement 3
Do you love warm weather, beautiful beaches, and friendly people? Then book a vacation with us to Tayrona National Park, in Colombia. Relax and enjoy the warm sun. The weather is always nice. There aren't any big hotels in the park, so go camping or stay in a small hotel. Don't visit the park in February. It usually closes for the month. Check our website to learn more.

9.2

1 very
2 wet
3 way
4 van
5 view
6 why

9.3

1 the ninth of January
2 the fifteenth of March
3 the twentieth of April
4 the tenth of October

UNIT 10

10.1

1 She's riding her bike in the park.
2 We're watching a movie on TV.
3 He's training for a marathon with his friend.
4 I'm buying some bananas in the market.

10.2

A: Thanks everyone for joining our Health at the Office workshop. Work's hard. That's why we call it "work"! It's sometimes stressful, but it's hard on your bodies, too. Sitting down all day isn't easy or good for you. It's important to move around. Let me start today by asking … how many of you do simple exercises at work?
B: Hmm. I'm at my desk all day. I usually forget to get up and walk around. But right now, I'm using my phone to help me remember. Every hour, it rings, and I go outside and climb up and down the stairs.
A: That's great. Anyone else?
C: Usually my body hurts after a day in my chair. But these days, I'm stretching more. Just a few simple exercises—raising my arms … touching my toes … It helps with my back.
A: Excellent. What about you back there?
D: I'm trying chair exercises. They're really easy. I like this one. I sit up straight, lift my right knee up, and keep it there for a few seconds. Then I do the same with my left knee.
A: Chair exercises. Perfect! That's what we're talking about today …

10.3

1 Go left, and then walk straight.
2 Go straight, turn right at the bank, and walk straight to the market.
3 Turn left at the high school, walk for 100 meters, and turn right.
4 Drive to the park, turn left at the lake, and continue for two kilometers.

Audioscripts

9&10 REVIEW 5

🎧 R5.1

Tour guide

Welcome everyone to our bus tour of Athens. It's an amazing city, and there's lots to do and see.

We start our tour at the National Gardens of Athens. There are many things to do here. This beautiful garden has benches for picnics. It also has a small zoo where you can visit the animals! Walk around and get some exercise. Take some pictures as you walk around the beautiful garden …

We're now stopping at the Panathenaic Stadium, the only stadium in the world built out of only marble. This is where the first Olympic Games were held in 1896. It is one of the city's famous spots. Do you see the people up on those steps right now? They are walking and enjoying the view. If you are feeling fit, you can climb up and join them! The stadium now has 50,000 seats …

We're now coming up to the National Library of Greece. There are more than one million books here! There are many beautiful sights to see here. It's a great place to take photos, but please try to be quiet …

🎧 R5.2

1 four
2 thirteen
3 eighteenth
4 twentieth

🎧 R5.3

1 Go to the café, turn left, then turn right.
2 Walk that way, turn right, and go straight.
3 Go straight, turn left at the movie theater, and turn left again at the park.
4 Turn left, turn right at the library, and go straight on Main Street.

UNIT 11

🎧 11.1

1 I was happy.
2 Were they at home?
3 Yes, they were.
4 Yes, she was.

🎧 11.2

Rhys: Hey, Caroline. Who are you listening to? Caroline?
Caroline: Oh, sorry, Rhys. What was that?
Rhys: Who are you listening to?
Caroline: Ali Farka Touré.
Rhys: Who's that? I don't know him.
Caroline: He was a musician from Mali. He was born in a small village near Timbuktu. He was a singer, but he played many musical instruments. He was fantastic on the guitar! His album *Talking Timbuktu* sold 238,000 copies in the U.S. and at least 100,000 copies throughout Europe!
Rhys: Cool.
Caroline: Yeah. His life was very interesting. He was a musician, but he was also a farmer. When he wasn't making music, he was usually on his farm near Timbuktu.
Rhys: Really?
Caroline: Yeah. He died in 2006. He was just 66 years old. I'm listening to his last album.
Rhys: When was that?
Caroline: In 2006—the year he died.
Rhys: Interesting. Can I have a listen?

🎧 11.3

1
A I'll see you at the museum tomorrow?
B Oh, no …
2
A Jenny wants to meet on Wednesday.
B No way!
3
A Here is your exam score.
B Interesting!
4
A Terry wants to talk to you.
B Really?

UNIT 12

1 boy   how
2 here   dear
3 now   out
4 toy   wow

A: Something funny happened to me last week. I woke up an hour late for class. I was really worried.

B: Oh, no! What did you do?

A: I didn't have breakfast or take a shower. I just changed my clothes and ran to the bus stop. I waited a long time for the bus, and it finally arrived. I got on, sat down, and just looked out the window and waited for the trip to end.

B: What time did you get to the university?

A: I got off the bus at 10:30—an hour late for class. I ran from the bus stop to the university. I was so hot and tired when I got there.

B: Was your teacher angry?

A: That's the thing. When I got there, the school was empty.

B: Really? Where was everyone?

A: I didn't know. So I took out my phone to call a classmate. And then I saw it, in big letters on my phone. It was Saturday!

1 Did it rain?
2 Did he cook this?
3 Where did they walk?
4 Why did she say that?
5 Did you enjoy it?

11&12 REVIEW 6

A: Hi, Natasha. Why are you smiling?

B: Something funny happened to me. I was just over at Ken's desk …

A: The new guy in your team? He's very friendly.

B: Well, I asked him to make 100 copies of a form for me.

A: And?

B: Well, he didn't make 100 copies.

A: How many copies did he make?

B: He only made 50 copies.

A: Oh. Did you say anything?

B: I did. I said I needed 100 copies, not 50. He said he was very sorry. Guess what he did next.

A: I'm terrible at guessing. What did he do?

B: He threw the 50 copies in the recycling bin! Then he went and made 100 new copies.

A: No way!

B: I didn't say anything. I just smiled at him and said "Thank you."

A: Were you at the meeting?

B: Yes, we were.

A: Was it interesting?

B: It was.

1 Did she like it?
2 What did you say?
3 Did they see me?
4 Where did he go?

Irregular verbs

BASE VERB	SIMPLE PAST		BASE VERB	SIMPLE PAST
be	was/were		make	made
become	became		meet	met
begin	began		pay	paid
bring	brought		put	put
build	built		read	read
buy	bought		ride	rode
choose	chose		run	ran
can	could		say	said
come	came		see	saw
do	did		sell	sold
drink	drank		send	sent
drive	drove		sing	sang
eat	ate		sit	sat
feel	felt		sleep	slept
find	found		speak	spoke
fly	flew		stand (up)	stood (up)
forget	forgot		swim	swam
get	got		take	took
give	gave		teach	taught
go	went		tell	told
have	had		think	thought
hold	held		understand	understood
keep	kept		wake (up)	woke (up)
know	knew		wear	wore
leave	left		win	won
lose	lost		write	wrote

Pronunciation chart

VOWELS

iː eat	ɪ it	ʊ put	uː blue
e leg	ə the	ɜː her	ɔː for
æ hat	ʌ but	ɑː car	ɒ from*

DIPHTHONGS

ɪə hear*	eɪ take	
ʊə tourist*	ɔɪ toy	əʊ old
eə where*	aɪ why	aʊ how

CONSONANTS

p pay	b buy	t talk	d day	tʃ cheap	dʒ jam	k cap	g get
f for	v vet	θ think	ð that	s sell	z zero	ʃ she	ʒ vision
m my	n near	ŋ long	h hot	l like	r right	w way	j yellow

voiced

unvoiced

* mainly used in British English

97

Notes

Notes

Notes

Notes

Notes

Notes

Notes

Credits